THE ETERNAL YEW

THE ETERNAL YEW

Trevor Baxter

MBE MIEH FRSA

Published in 1992 by
The Self Publishing Association Ltd
Units 7/10, Hanley Workshops,
Hanley Swan, Worcs.
A MEMBER OF

in association with
TREVOR BAXTER

British Library Cataloguing in Publication Data

A catalogue record for this book is available from
The British Library

ISBN 1 85421 148 X

Designed & Produced by Images Design & Print Ltd, Hanley Swan, Worcs.
Printed and Bound in Great Britain by Hartnolls Ltd, Bodmin, Cornwall.

Contents

List of Illustrations

To the Memory of

HARRY BAXTER

who gave me a life long interest in trees.

The trunk of the Brockenhurst Yew.

ACKNOWLEDGEMENTS

One of the abiding features of my travels in search of Yew lore in all its various guises is the amount of goodwill generated by the project. The wealth of interest and cooperation extended to and encompassed almost every conceivable set of circumstances.

In addition to the people I have specifically mentioned in the text it is my pleasure to acknowledge the assistance and goodwill I have received from the following:

Dennis Smale, Frontispiece, Hambledon Hill 70, Tarrant Rushton 24.

Jon Stone, Great Yew Wood 62-63, Selborne Yew 130-131.

Gordon Brand, Irish – Florence Court, Ulster 51.

James Clevett, Kingley Vale Forest 58 & 60.

Peter Howarth, Plate No 8, 37.

Cynthia Sansom, Yew carving 176.

Colin Bacon, Harlington Church Yew 166.

Rev. David Brewster, 1850 print. Brockenhurst Church & Yew 151.

Chris Bell, Dovaston Yew 55, Eastham Yew 168-169, Gresford Yew 155.

Westmorland Gazette, Levens Hall 95.

The National Trust, Crom Castle 74.

Ernest Newbury, Churchyard Yew, Didcot 171.

I also wish to thank those who have so readily given information in letters, or in person and have invariably concluded by wishing the project every success, they include:

Irene von Prondzynski, Ron and Brenda Chappell, Pamela Cook, Cheryl Bates, Faith Harris, Mona Evans, Barbara Spencer, Margaret Lees, Liz Foulkes, Barbara Botting, James Perks, Malcolm Perks, Frank Hewitson, Charles E. Pringle, Arther Day, Mr. J.R. Freeman, Mr. F. Cope and Mr & Mrs B. Watson & Mr Walley.

In addition to the many clergymen mentioned in the text I wish to thank:

Rev'ds M.J. Pomeroy, J.R.P. Ashby, D. Meara, D. Streater, P.S.G. Hoyle, T.E. Yates, I.D. Gardner, M.M. Edge, G. Sidaway, D. Partridge and Canon A. Redman.

HISTORICAL

ASSOCIATIONS

Yew Trees at Fountains Abbey, Yorkshire.

This group of Yews were well known for the shelter they gave to workers on the Abbey Estate. Unfortunately they suffered considerable storm damage and were subsequently removed.

Chapter One

It is Harvest Sunday, and the Village church, bedecked with country produce, is the day's focal point for young and old. A spirit of goodwill overlays the scene; little knots of people exchange pleasantries as they walk beneath the massive spread of the Churchyard Yew.

The dense umbrella of dusky green leaves tends to create a rather special localised atmosphere. The unique scarlet fruits are highlighted by the evening sun, and within the crown of the Yew oblique shafts of sunlight filter through the chequer-work of branches. In response, the well-worn flags display a dappled pattern of muted light which gives way to dark shade around the huge bole of the tree.

Although it is the time of the year when most trees are closing down for Winter, the Yew presents a striking display, inviting us to take a closer look at one of our most fascinating native trees. Perhaps because these venerable Yews have always been there, their presence in this timeless scene and their living link with a bygone age is often overlooked or at least taken for granted. It is however, clearly remarkable that the present day families attending the Village Church are seeing the same living scene as their great Grandparents saw, and much the same living scene as their great Grandchildren are likely to see. Such is the nature of Yew trees, that six generations will make no significant difference to their appearance. Unchanging in a changing world, they are a unique part of our living heritage, giving the countryside and the Country Church a sense of stability, peace and tranquillity.

Through many centuries the Yew has gained a distinctive role in our history, poetry and folklore. The story of this tree is like a chart of Great Britain and Ireland from Pre-Christian times onwards. In a primitive and pagan Britain the Yew's very early history is lost in antiquity, but certain factors point the way to the special relationship between the Yew and early Man.

It was a period when large areas of the country were covered by forests, in which the Yew and the Oak were particularly prominent. There were several native evergreens, including holly and juniper, but only the Yew, with its dense foliage, and apparent immortality, had the role of a protective deity. This early religious significance was, in all probability, the tree's initial association with spiritual beliefs throughout the ages.

One of the earliest uses of Yew wood was to make small boards, inscribed with runic letters. This primitive alphabet was often used to call for the assistance of supernatural powers in some specific task. There is evidence of frequent use of these boards in Celtic and Irish folklore, and they were subsequently known as "magic wands", their use extending into Christian times.

English and Welsh history records that Yew trees in certain locations were consecrated and held sacred; this special recognition was in the nature of a tree preservation order. It was also an important link in the evolution of the Yew tree's relationship with the churchyard. It seems clear that some of the sites of pagan worship were taken over upon the advent of Christianity, and the Yews on these sites may well have been the forerunners of the Churchyard Yew. Saxon and Medieval circular churchyards often appear to be a continuation of use of an ancient circular mound or stockade, left from a time when the veneration of trees was part of the cult of nature worship.

The Church dedicated to St Elli at Llanelly, Gilwern, Gwent is an example of this, and other sites in Kent and at Brockenhurst, Hampshire show indications of having been sacred spots in Pre-Christian times. At Llanelly the church stands within a circle of 16 Yews; 13 are ancient Yews, which may even be older than the present thirteenth century church. Mr T. Conrad Williams, The Rector's Warden, was able to tell me that the three younger Yews were replacements for losses through storm damage in 1947.

In some instances where an ancient Yew is situated alongside the path to the entrance to a medieval Church, it may well be that the Yew tree pre-dates the earliest part of the existing building and invariably provides a link with a vanished era. The symbolic unbroken sequence

16

continues today, as Yews are still being planted.

Festival and funeral rites figure predominantly in the early history of the Yew. The seemingly endless life of the churchyard Yew led to the custom of Yew Sprays being carried above the coffin to the Church for the funeral service, and subsequently buried with the body as a symbol of resurrection and immortality. A further occasional practice was to rub the corpse with an infusion of Yew leaves.

It became common practice for Yew sprays to be carried in procession on Palm Sunday, and during Passion Week they were used to decorate the crucifix in Irish homes.

The exalted position of immortality did not prevent some poets expressing adverse sentiments about the Churchyard Yew; hopefully, these are balanced by other poets expressing its virtues.

Mystical associations are also hidden in the ritual of the fiery Yew cross used by Scottish clans as a rallying signal to all members of the clan.

The fiery Yew Cross carried as a rallying signal to gather the Clan.

Sir Walter Scott described it in *The Lady of the Lake:*

A slender crosslet formed with care
A cubit's length in measure due;
The shaft and limbs were rods of Yew.

The Midnight Magic of Yew is recalled by Shakespeare in *Macbeth*.

Liver of blaspheming Jew
Gall of goat and slips of Yew,
Slivered in the moon's eclipse.

Many village stories refer to the Churchyard Yew at midnight as a place to be left alone.

Thomas Stanley, a mid 17th Century poet, writes in mournful terms of the practice of strewing graves with Yew:

Yet strew upon my grave
Such offerings as you have
Forsaken Cypresses and sad Yew,
For kinder flowers can take no birth
Or growth from such unhappy earth.

Matthew Arnold preferred the transient gaiety of the rose:

Strew on her roses, roses
And never a spray of Yew;
In quiet she reposes;
And would that I did too.

The poet Blair addressed the Churchyard Yew in parody:

Cheerless unsociable plant!
That loves to dwell
Mid'st skulls and coffins,
Epitaphs and worms.

Tennyson in particular was very gloomy:

Old Yew which graspest at the stones
That name the underlying dead,
Thy fibres net the dreamless head,
Thy roots are wrapt about the bones.

Dark Yew that graspeth at the stones.

Oh not for thee the glow, the bloom,
Who changest not in any gale!
Nor branding summer suns avail
To touch thy thousand years of gloom.

Thomas Gray in his *Elegy, Written in a Country Churchyard*, was also melancholy:

Beneath those rugged Elms, that Yew-tree's shade
Where heaves the turf in many a mouldering heap
Each in his narrow cell for ever laid
The rude forefathers of the hamlet sleep.

Herrick was mindful of the Cypresse and Yew in funeral rites, and requested both to honour his tomb:

Both of you have relation to the grave;
And where the funeral trump sounds you are there

I shall be made ere long a fleeting shade;
Pray come, and do some honour to my tomb,
Do not deny my last request, for I will be
Thankful to you, or friends to me.

Perhaps I can redress the balance a little towards the more genial look at the Churchyard Yew, by the inclusion of a poem which has found favour in National and Regional magazines. Clearly I came upon the Churchyard Yew at Broadwell in the Cotswolds in different circumstances.

THE CHURCHYARD YEW

The eternal Yew witness of an epoch past
Host to transient mortals with their fleeting joy
And sadness to which the memory clings,
A link with bowmakers of a bygone age,
A link with knights and noblemen
Their deeds enshrined by tablets on the wall.
Aside the mellow church
Brooding at nightfall with an air of mystery,
Paying homage to the barn owl
Motionless, yet scanning his domain
Displayed by fitful moonlight
Through broken cloud beyond the lantern tower.

Around the fluted bole, there is shelter from the midday sun,
A hint of darkness through the day.
But on those spreading boughs the dancing leaves unveil
A dappled interplay of light and shade,
A moving pattern on a well-worn path
Enriched by nature's palette of lacy lichen tints
Unsullied in the country air.
As summer ebbs away the broad leaves fall,
The Yew, now glistening in the autumn scene
Puts on her show of scarlet fruit for song birds
To match the harvest hymns.
Unyielding to the sighing winds of winter
Until the lengthening days usher in spring flowers

Churchyard Yew at Broadwell, Gloucestershire.

Primrose and periwinkle to grace the Yew tree scene
Soon the pace of nature quickens, the scents of May abound,
First light is early, sundown is late
And dark green buds are tipped a paler hue.

And now that special day is here,
The bells ring out a happy sound,
The village band appears, their instruments all shining bright

The rector is walking and warden too
Church banners are high and waving in the breeze,
Then comes a precious moment in life's time,
Listen to that blissful sound a-drifting
O'er the green
Children are singing,
Now coming into view,
They are walking past the churchyard Yew.

The Churchyard Yew is also present in a poem I wrote in connection with a railway magazine article on memories of a country station.

Country station in the vale,
The sidings now beset with willow herb and rusting rail
Quiet as the Churchyard
Platforms bare, silence and stillness everywhere

Station memories of parting sadness
Of joyful meetings and instant gladness
Of early morning milk trains everyday
Of cattle trucks on market day

Station memories of the overnight mail speeding through,
And the fleeting firebox light on the church's sable Yew.
The faint tremble of the window frame
And then the haunting sound of the distant train.

Walter De La Mare also had a special word the the Yew tree in his poem *Trees:*

Of all the trees in England
Oak, Elder, Elm and Thorn
The Yew alone burns lamps of peace
For them that lie forlorn.

UNIQUE GROWTH

STYLE OF THE YEW

The Churchyard Yew at Tarrant Rushton, Dorset
showing more than a hollow centre.

Chapter Two

In large areas of the United Kingdom and Ireland there exists a range of Churchyard Yews of infinite shape and size. The typical ancient Yew will have a short bole of six to ten feet with several massive branches – some almost horizontal, extending up to 25 feet – and a veritable maze of smaller branches. The total spread of the branches may cover up to one quarter of an acre, and the tree may be twenty to fifty feet high. In addition to the identifying characteristics in terms of leaf and fruit, the Yew bole is also unmistakable with its thin flaky bark, mid-brown in colour, with light brown patches where the bark has recently been shed.

When a mature Yew has to be felled it is not uncommon for the bark line of the main branches to extend three or more feet into the body of the bole to reveal the points where the single trunk changed to a multiple or compound trunk. In these circumstances the width of planking available from the tree is invariably less than anticipated.

Occasionally one sees in an old churchyard what initially appears to be several trees of varying size set roughly in a ring or part of a ring, of eight to ten feet in diameter. They are likely to be the peripheral remains of an ancient Yew planted between 800 to 1600 years ago, the heart of the tree having decayed and completely vanished.

The peripheral growth of the typical short Yew bole develops an irregular fluted or buttressed pattern. The nature of this unique style of growth is dealt with in detail because it is of major significance in the estimation of the age of the tree, which is a perennial pastime for many dendrologists. A variety of formulae have been put forward as methods of calculation. Although information on planting dates is scarce, the available evidence points to a very large number of Churchyard Yews being within an age range of 400 to 1000 years, with some exceptional examples beyond this range. Clearly Yew trees have a life-span well beyond all other native trees.

The usual practice is to measure the girth at a convenient height, preferably three to four feet from the ground, ascertain the diameter from this measurement, and then deduce the number of annual growth rings assumed to be necessary to produce a tree of that diameter.

Girth measurements need to be considered in conjunction with

a) a close scrutiny of the trunk. Is it hollow, forked or compound and to what extent has it generated new and independent growth from the root stock or the base of the trunk?

b) the girth of the main branches in relation to the girth of the trunk. Do they spring from the crown, or partially intact crown, or from the periphery of the remains of the trunk, or from new growth which has intermingled and virtually coalesced with the older parts of the trunk?

c) site location, ground condition, general vitality of the tree, extent of the umbrage and the sex.

Scientific assistance in the form of carbon dating has in some instances been used; the prime aim is to find and test the oldest piece of Yew wood obtained from the interior of a hollow tree. Most Yew trees are hollow at 400 years and almost all at 700, so Yew wood beyond this age is not likely to exist.

Other aids which have been used to ascertain the age of a Yew include obtaining the average of several bore-hole core samples to indicate approximate growth rates at particular periods within the life of the Yew. Similarly, samples of decayed wood from the inside of a hollow tree will provide ring counts indicating the growth rate of that part of the tree. There are however so many variables and peculiarities of growth applicable to Yew trees that no general formula can be put forward as a panacea to end all speculative assessment. This is due to the absence of information about the growth pattern of the hollow portion which on many ancient Yew trees will be several times greater in area than the portion of the trunk which is still intact.

The hollow portion may vary from a horseshoe-shaped area set out with bench-type seating for twelve people as provided for in the

Churchyard Yew, Much Marcle, Nr. Hereford, providing seating for twelve people.

Churchyard Yew at Much Marcle, to a comparatively small area as in the Yews at Stowting, and Monks Horton in Kent where the hollow centre has become partially filled in with a new secondary trunk. This type of growth will not be recorded by girth measurements and accordingly is likely to be the reason for apparently insignificant growth over a long period.

Although this infilling is not exceptional, the bulk of new growth which occurs in ancient Yews usually takes place on the periphery of the trunk rather than the hollow interior. This type of confused growth will continue over centuries to give the appearance of a single deeply buttressed trunk. In some instances new growth will intermingle and flow around the remains of the original trunk.

Only a reliable date of planting can give conclusive evidence of age. estimates based on other factors can only be a rough guide. The basic problem of age estimation often arises comparatively early in the life of the Yews, and it is further complicated by the fact that each tree is unique.

At an early age, one or more core points within the trunk, begins to develop. Each core point is the start of a separate growth pattern, and may result in a twin trunk; several core points would generate their own concentric ring growth. Meanwhile the all-enveloping circular rings on the periphery of the multi-or compound trunk continue to grow in a conventional way as though the new growth points did not exist. This confused growth pattern continues particularly in   trees where a century or more may pass before the break-up of the trunk into separate branches is complete.

Unfortunately their conventional early growth permits water and debris to collect in pockets in the crown of the trunk, and the water seeps down the interior of the trunk via the partially separate components leading eventually to the decay of the interior.

Externally there may be no obvious indication of the nature of the compound trunk, although in many instances a buttressed appearance and the increased girth (e.g. at 6 feet from ground level when compared with 2 feet) will indicate the effect of the multiplicity of growth rings.

Sections of a Yew trunk will reveal whether it is a single trunk, twin

This multi-trunk Yew has produced a ring of secondary trunks of various shapes and sizes. With this type of growth pattern it is likely that within the latter half of the 21st century the continuous growth on the periphery will have eliminated the deep fissures between the component parts of the multi-trunk. It will then tend to present the appearance of a massive single trunk. This tree is a typical churchyard Yew capable of continuous life. The three limitations to life which it faces are severe storm damage, extensive decay within the trunk due to water and fungal attack, the water seeping down from pockets at the crown of the trunk, and weakness due to a lack of soil nutrients to maintain a healthy growth. All three dangers can be minimized by an appropriate maintenance programme. As regards growth pattern the difference between this type of growth and that of a typical single trunk Yew at Buckland Monochorum on page no 104 is immediately noticeable.

PLATE 1

Section of 78 years old Yew trunk 1ft 10ins girth. The nature of the unusual ring formation is in preparation for a change from a single trunk to a multi-trunk. In this tree the rate of diametric growth increased three fold after reaching the age of 35 years, and continued at this rate for 17 years, thereafter reverting to its earlier growth rate.

PLATE 2

The same Yew has now produced four core points to start a multi-trunk Yew. Voids are starting to appear between the partially separte trunks.

31

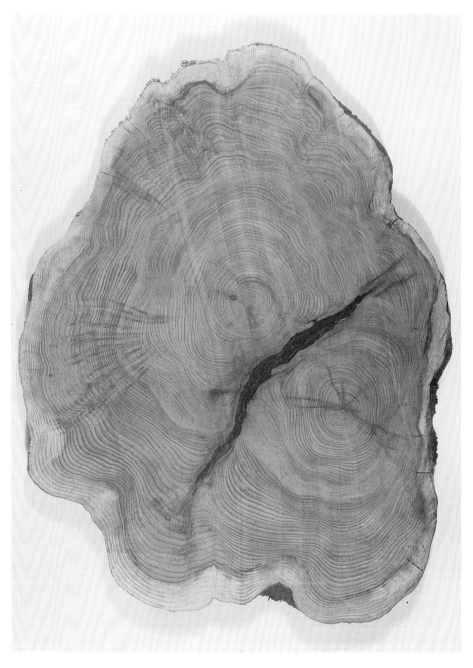

PLATE 3

A 122 year old twin trunk still enclosed by an all enveloping annular ring growth on the periphery of the trunk, the girth 4 feet 7 inches.

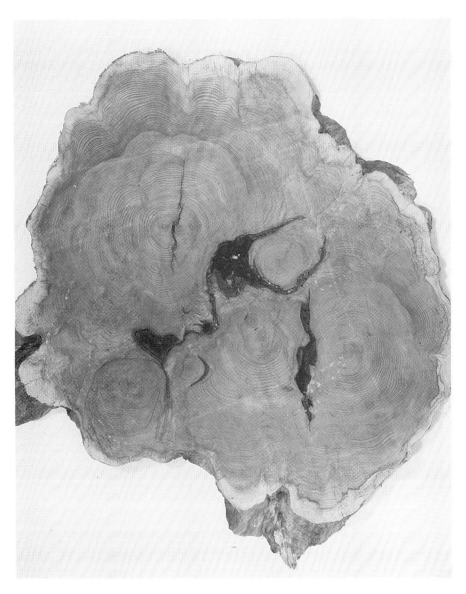

PLATE 4

A 122 year old multi-trunk Yew from the same wood. This yew is in the process of dividing into 10 trunks, and substantial voids have appeared. They will eventually become filled with water and debris from the crown of the tree 6 feet above. A situation which is conducive to decay and ultimately a hollow trunk. At this stage of growth there is still 7 inches to 1 foot 2 inches of solid wood continuing to grow and enclose the multi-trunk growth in an all enveloping annular ring structure in the periphery. The girth is 8 feet, almost twice the girth of the twin trunk Yew of similar age shown on Plate 3.

33

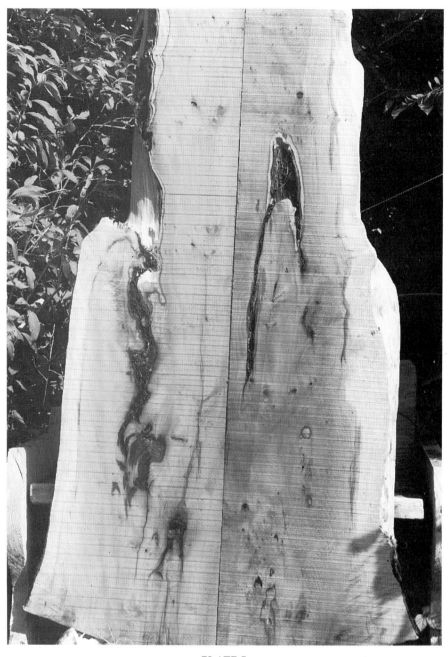

PLATE 5

(Plates 5 & 6.) Longitudinal sections showing the inevitable voids in a multi-trunk tree which severely limits the quantity of useful timber.

PLATE 6

PLATE 7

Shows the eccentric growth which is often produced within the confines of a multi-trunk where growth is predominantly towards the periphery of a milti-trunk Yew.

PLATE 8

A tall single trunk Yew grown in favourable conditions on the Knockdrin Estate, Co. Westmeath. 224 years old 10ft 10ins girth.

The patchy staining is due to the trunk lying on the woodland floor amidst dense undergrowth for several years.

trunk, or multi-trunk and if the latter, the various stages before complete separation can be observed. After separation the continuing growth is such that *interlocking and overlapping occurs to maintain the impression of a* single trunk. No other tree can be so misleading in appearance than an old Yew tree.

It is so easy to think that the massive trunk is derived solely from the continuous addition of annual growth rings to the periphery.

The plates showing various sections of Yew trunks illustrate the above points.

The competition for space results in the new growth areas of the compound trunk being pressed against each other in the central area with virtually no room for growth. Sometimes there are as many as 80 growth rings per inch. The peripheral growth in these circumstances is often between eight and twelve rings per inch but other factors may influence this. In very old trees new growth on the periphery increases the chaotic structure of the Yew; it continues in a distorted fashion, overlapping and flowing around areas of slower growth and appearing to actually fuse and coalesce. This bolstering up process produces great strength, and even hollow trees may support a massive array of branches leaving the crown of the bole at widely varying angles.

In woodlands, rare instances occur where Yew seeds have germinated in a very localised sheltered situation. In such circumstances and over a long period of years, they may abut each other and continue to grow in a manner which gives the impression of a single tree.

This situation is extremely unusual in Churchyard Yews. However, Reg Wheeler, a retired forester, has made an extensive survey of Churchyard Yews in Central and North Wales. He noted a Yew in the Churchyard at St Erfyl Llanerfyl which a local writer had earlier considered to be three trunks from a single rootstock, but was in fact two separate trees and possibly three. He deduced this from the absence of a single trunk at ground level, the difference in sex and other characteristics of growth. In this instance their location in a very prominent place in the churchyard would seem to indicate a definite planting rather than a natural occurrence.

Growth patterns are also greatly influenced by location and soil condition. A thin soil which over a century or more has lost much of its nutrient value is not the ideal place to keep a large Yew in good health. The size and quality of the crown of the tree are good indications of the soil quality.

An example of an extremely vigorous Yew tree stands within the landscaped gardens of Shugborough, Staffordshire. It is referred to in detail in the chapter on Country House Yews.

Yew trees over forty feet in height with a single clean trunk to fifteen feet or more are not unusual, but are usually found in Yew avenues, courtyards and parklands. These tall clean trunk Yews drift into a position of virtually no growth and thin umbrage. Their apparent inability to generate new growth from the base, means they will never reach the age of the venerable Yews which grace our churchyards.

The finest examples are in Close Walk Woods at Cowdray. Whilst the woodland situation tends to enhance this type of growth it would seem to be only a secondary factor, since the ancient Yews at Kingley Vale are also in dense woodland, but are more akin to the typical churchyard Yew with massive branches at a comparatively low level.

After the hazards of estimating the age of ancient hollow Yews and also those with compound trunks, it would seem that estimating the age of a single trunk Yew with a diameter of around one foot would be an easy task. However, even a ready made formula for Yews of this size can be misleading. This is largely due to the substantial difference in the rate of growth of Yew trees even when planted at the same time and in close proximity as in avenue and terrace situations. The difference in girth is such that comparatively young trees will give measurements more then twice that of an adjacent tree of the same age. The ninety-nine Yew trees planted in Painswick Churchyard show a girth difference range of this ratio. Similar variations have been noted in the Great Yew Forest at Kingley Vale near Chichester, at Blickling Hall, Norfolk and Daylesford, Gloucestershire.

There is a continuous loss of ancient Yew trees and it is not uncommon to see others in a state of decline. These trees are part of our history, a living history. A modest maintenance programme such as a quinquennial inspection by a dendrologist followed by appropriate action to prevent or arrest decline and decay is worthwhile. There is little doubt that in some instances the application of suitable soil nutrients to replace those depleted by centuries of growth would enhance the life of an ancient Yew and reverse its decline. Ground aeration where necessary, sterilant treatment to avoid fungal attacks to damp hollow areas in the trunk, all need to be given proper consideration. It is not uncommon to see chains and supports placed in position more than one hundred years ago, which are now serving no useful purpose because of changes in growth patterns; some chains are partly buried in a branch and doing more harm than good.

An assessment of the likely ability of the tree to withstand gale force winds is also essential. It may be prudent to carry out a degree of modest lopping, particularly of long horizontal and other branches capable of exerting excessive stresses within or near the trunk.

Perhaps we are less rewarded by endeavouring to ascertain whether the vanished heartwood of an old Yew had its origin 700 or 1000 years ago, than by successfully campaigning for and obtaining adequate maintenance for these trees. The decline of an ancient Yew can invariably be arrested and its life rejuvenated so other generations can then continue to enjoy the mystery of its longevity.

Yew tree in the churchyard at Todenham, Gloucestershire.
This 21ft 6ins girth Yew tree shows the typical multi-trunk growth pattern.

BOTANICAL

FEATURES

Terminal buds on a female yew distorted and destroyed by the larva of the Yew gnat.

Chapter Three

The Common Yew, *Taxus Baccata*, is one of only three native conifers, the other two being Scots Pine and Juniper. The botanic name *TAXUS* is from the Latin and Greek for the tree. Although still widespread in Southern England, its numbers are in decline and new planting is not keeping place with losses.

The leaves are evergreen, less than one inch in length, very narrow with recurved edges and a prominent central vein. The Yew is normally doiecious – each tree is distinctly male or female – but a number of instances may be noted where one branch will have the characteristics of the opposite sex. The outstanding difference from other members of the Coniferae family is in the character of the fruit, the ripe seed being surrounded by a red fleshy aril, popularly known as the berry. The male flowers consist of a tiny stalk with a bulbous head of 6 to 12 stamens; attached to each stamen are approximately 6 pollen sacs. The female flowers grow on the underside of the stem; they have the appearance of tiny olive green acorns sitting on a small disc. This acorn, like seed, is waiting for the right conditions, usually in March when the wind will carry the pollen from the male flowers. This phenomenon is appropriately highlighted by Tennyson in *The Holy Grail.*

> Beneath a world old Yew tree, darkening half
> The cloisters, on a gustful April morn,
> That puffed the swaying branches into smoke.

Tennyson also refers to the dispersion of pollen in the following lines, which would be difficult to understand without prior knowledge of Yew flowers.

> Old warder of these buried bones,
> And answering now my random stroke;

Wind dispersal of Yew pollen.
(with fruitful cloud and living smoke)

Dark Yew that graspeth at the stones
And dippest towards the dreamless head
With fruitful cloud and living smoke:
To thee too, comes the golden hour,
When flower is feeling after flower

Whereas the seeds of the Ash, Sycamore and Oak seem almost anxious to germinate, Yew seeds which germinate in the wild need to be in a suitable sheltered damp spot, free from all the hazards which make it difficult for a seedling of very slow growth to become established.

There is satisfaction in growing Yew from seed and the following method has proved successful. Collect the ripe berries in the Autumn, clear the pulp by washing the seed with four times their bulk of sand; then bury the tray for twelve to fourteen months. This rest period seems to suit the Yew seed which can then be sown about two inches apart in rich loamy soil and covered by half an inch of friable soil. This does not usually produce mass germination; some will come up in the Spring, others will wait to the following year.

The young Yews are so small and slow growing that they may give the appearance of failing but this is not the case. A little care and protection in the seed bed for two or three years, will prepare them for transplanting.

Poisonous nature of the Yew Spray

Yew leaves and seeds contains the poison Taxin, an alkaloid, which if eaten in sufficient quantity is fatal to horses, cattle, pigs, sheep, goat and dogs. Horses are particularly vulnerable and special care is needed where paddocks and gallops adjoin woodlands containing Yew trees.

However, some farmers have reported that Yew leaves eaten in small quantities on more than one occasion has not produced any noticeable effect on farm animals in their care.

Children are attracted to the red berries of the Yew. In the olden days it was commonplace for children to pick the berries and eat them. Whilst the red mucilage or pulp surrounding the seeds are not poisonous, the seeds are and accordingly children should be made aware of the dangers of eating them.

It has always been known that Yew leaves are poisonous to humans.

> At least three deaths from eating Yew leaves have been recorded at Coroners inquests during the past two years, two in Derbyshire and one in London. In each case substantial quantity of Yew leaves had been eaten.
>
> At the London inquest medical evidence revealed that the death was due to alkaloid poisoning.
>
> The effects of poisoning include vomiting, muscular weakness, coma and convulsions which may result in heart and respitatory failure and possibly death.

Farmers and gamekeepers have occasionally reported the death of pheasants from eating Yew leaves; other farmers have noted that poultry turkeys and peacocks have eaten Yew leaves without ill effects. No doubt the quantity of leaves eaten is an important factor.

However, to the thrush and the blackbird, Autumn is akin to a very long birthday. These song birds have a particular liking for the sweet red mucilage and eat large quantities. The seeds are discarded or passed through the digestive system. At Todenham, Gloucestershire, I noticed that Yew seedlings are very common in cottage gardens near to the Churchyard Yew.

Another aspect of the use of the Yew tree is worthy of note. Recent developments in medicine have shown its value as an aid to the healing process. The formation of scar tissue is part of this process, but when it appears in the eye it can cause very restricted vision. This is one of the problems faced by patients recovering from an eye injury; scar tissue is formed by cells multiplying and then contracting rapidly to form a toughened mass. This happens in the eye in the same way as anywhere else in the body; the consequences can be a serious problem. However, researchers have reported that a substance called Taxol extracted from the Yew has prevented cell contraction and has had no toxic effects.

A young Yew tree at Todenham, Gloucestershire which seems determined to succeed in spite of being sown by a bird in a difficult position adjacent to a substantial tree.

Disease and Pests

Laetiporous Sulphureus is usually the fungus responsible for the decay of Yew wood, but *Coniophora Cerebella* and *Creolophus Cirrhatus* can occasionally be seen present in the interior of hollow Yew trees where dampness and debris also hasten the decay process. No doubt other pathogens contribute to the ill health of Yew trees; disease can enter the tree through the cut ends of lopped branches. As a preservative measure, these branch ends should be sealed with a sterilant, to keep the tree in a state of full vigour.

Forty years ago this Yew tree was in good health, it is now a dying shell displaying a subtantial amount of fungus growth.

Unlike Oak, the Yew has very few parasites. A common pest is *Cecidomyia Taxi*, a tiny gnat which lays its eggs in the Yew tree bud. The reddish tinted larvae cause the bud to enlarge with immature leaves which do not develop. In shape the distorted bud resembles a tiny artichoke. It does not however appear to do any significant damage to the tree, unless the infection is widespread and a substantial number of terminal buds are destroyed.

A young Yew supporting two types of litchen.

Yew Cultivars

The two main cultivars of The Common Yew (*Taxus Baccata*) are the Irish Yew (*Taxus Baccata Fastigiata*) and the Dovaston Yew (*Taxus Baccata Dovastoniana*).

The Irish Yew (Taxus Baccata Fastigiata)

Undoubtedly the Irish Yew is the next most important member after the Common Yew; its origin as a distinct form found growing wild in Ireland and its subsequent history are quite fascinating.

It is a somewhat smaller tree and although classified as being of upright or fastigiate growth, it is unique in many ways. When young, the upright growth of its branches together with the absence of bulk of any significance gives it a columnar outline; with further growth towards maturity it becomes a tall dense tree of elliptical shape.

Continuous new growth on the perimeter increases the width to the extent that in the absence of trimming, a mature tree will have the appearance of a huge cylindrical bush with a flattish top. When several are planted in churchyards to line the path to the church they make a notable contribution to the scene.

In large country house gardens the Irish Yew is often planted as a single distinctive tree to mark a particular point such as the end of a terrace or the entrance to a glade or alley. The golden variety is a striking ornamental tree which adds a special interest and colour to the garden.

The Irish Yew was originally known as the Florence Court Yew and is still occasionally referred to by that name. The circumstances of its discovery at Florence Court, County Fermanagh is a captivating event in the long history of the Yew tree. The Countess of Enniskillen in her writings on *Florence Court My Irish Home* gave a fascinating insight to the discovery of the Irish Yew. The story of the find is also well documented by local writers.

It was in the year 1767 that George Willis, a tenant farmer of Ahitirourke, was out in search of hares on the mountainous area above

The original Irish Yew at Florence Court, Enniskillen, Northen Ireland.

Florence Court. As he was passing the rocks called Carrig-na-madadh, now known locally as Willis rock, he noticed two very young Yew trees. Their columnar appearance attracted him; he dug them up, and took them back to his farm.

He planted one in his own garden and took the other in his poacher-type coat pocket to his landlord, Baron Mountflorence, who later became the first Earl of Enniskillen. This tree was planted near to Florence Court House where it is still living. This Yew, now 224 years old, is the parent tree of tens of thousands of Irish Yews scattered throughout the world. For many years it suffered damage through the incessant demand for cuttings for propagation in America and Europe. The tree which Mr Willis planted in his own garden died in 1865.

Florence Court is now a National Trust property, and is one of the most important houses in Ulster. Built in the mid 18th century, it contains some exceptionally fine rococo plasterwork. The setting is superb with fine views over surrounding mountains, and there are excellent walks in Florence Court park. Also of interest on the estate are the water wheel, hydraulic ram and the ice house. The original Florence Court Yew is marked with a special plaque outlining its history.

Gordon Brand, Administrator, Florence Court, has recently measured this Yew. These and earlier measurements are:

	1910	1990
Height	25 feet	33 feet
Circumference of branches	66 feet	84 feet
Circumference of twin trunks	43 inches and	77 inches and
	36 inches	67 inches

Over the past century, the Florence Court Yew has developed a looser habit of growth; this is noticeable in the photograph. Many of its offspring are around 30 feet in height and display a tighter columnar habit of growth as shown by the Irish Yews alongside a bridle path at Knockdrin Castle, near Mullingar, Westmeath, Ireland, and those at St Peters, Peterchurch, near Hereford.

Irish Yew alongside a bridle path at Knockdrin Castle, Co. Westmeath, Ireland.

The Dovaston Yew, Taxus Baccata Dovastoniana

The Dovaston Yew follows closely on the Irish Yew as an important and distinctive variety. There is further common ground in so far as the original tree is still thriving at well over 200 years old. It was bought from a pedlar at the door of Dovaston Hall, Westfelton, Shropshire about the year 1777. The tree, a fine specimen, has continuously been in good health. In 1880 the girth was 7 feet 10 inches; by 1900 it was 8 feet 10 inches and in 1988 12 feet four inches, at 212 years. The tree is attractive with long horizontal branches and pendulous branchlets. The tree is monoecious, one branch producing fertile seed which reproduced the form of the Dovaston Yew.

Dovaston Yews are no longer a rare variety but there is always the probability that fertilisation by a common Yew will not produce Dovaston Yews.

Dovaston Hall has been demolished and part of the estate developed for housing. Fortunately the original tree has been saved and will continue as a link with a past era.

There are attractive golden forms of *Taxus Baccata Fastigiata* and *Taxus Baccata Dovastonii*. In both forms the leaves have yellow margins. The latter was raised from a male clone of French origin.

Taxus Baccata Elegantissima is a golden bush frequently seen in garden centres; it is a dense bush with the young shoots a bright yellow. *Taxus Baccata Lutea* is the yellow berried Yew tree; the masses of yellow arils are quite spectacular. Originally discovered in 1817 at Glasnevin near Dublin, it is not uncommon in Ireland and is usually available from those nurseries which have a comprehensive tree list. Although the Yew genus is comparatively small, several intermediate forms have been developed by specialist nurserymen. The majority have an attractive golden or variegated form and nearly all are slow growing.

The original Dovaston Yew at Dovaston, West Felton, Shropshire.

Dovaston Yew – characteristic penulous branchlets.

THE YEW IN FOREST

AND WOODLAND

Ancient Yews in Kingley Vale Forest.

Chapter Four

Kingley Vale Yew Forest

There are very few Yew forests still in existence. Fortunately, the largest in Europe is delightfully situated at Kingley Vale on the South Downs above Chichester. This Yew forest is under the control of the Nature Conservancy Council whose warden is Richard Williamson, an author of distinction. Kingley Vale is unique. It is generally acknowledged to be one of the most beautiful and least known nature reserves under the control of the Council.

I met Richard Williamson at the field museum on the edge of the forest, and he was able to direct me to the group of ancient Yews which I particularly wanted to see. The visit was so rewarding that I returned to the site on two following days whilst staying at Bognor Regis. It is a completely different experience from the observation of a single ancient churchyard Yew or even a group of Yews as at Overton.

At Kingley Vale, it is not only the sheer mass of Yew trees which make the forest remarkable. It also possesses an atmosphere of eerie stillness and sinister quietude, unlike any other forest I have seen. Several forked and split trees with huge horizontal branches are grouped with other Yews of more conventional shape big enough to grace a churchyard scene. Undoubtedly it is their setting in the half light of the forest which gives them such a bewitching presence.

A massive Yew in Kingley Vale Forest.

Great Yews and Little Yew Woods, Nr Salisbury, Wiltshire

These ancient pure Yew woods close to the village of Odstock are within the estate of the Earl of Radnor. They are of exceptional historic importance. The Great Yews Wood covers 85 acres and it is mentioned in the Domesday Book as a place from which Yew wood was taken for long-bow making. The Little Yews Wood, although smaller in size, also contains some exceptionally fine Yews. The estate is managed by Mr Walley from the office at Longford Castle.

Close Walk Woods, Cowdray, Midhurst

The Yews in the avenue in Close Walk Woods are remarkable for their height; the tallest are around 80 feet. Recent storms have caused some damage, but they remain the tallest avenue in Europe.

Whereas the general growth pattern of the Yew in churchyards and parklands is that of a short trunk of 6 to 12 feet topped by a multi-branched crown, the Yews at Close Walk have clean trunks up to 24 feet with no large branches. One of the prime benefits of my Yew journeys is the inevitability of a meeting with someone who is helpful and happy to share information on Yew trees. My visit to Close Walks was no exception. In a pleasant discourse, Mr Maurice Smith of Close Walk outlined the history of the woods and their link with Cowdray. Their longevity and importance is reflected in past events which include the visit of Queen Elizabeth to the Yew avenues in 1591 whilst attending a banquet given by Viscount Montague. Unfortunately, there is little doubt that the maintenance and care of the wood during the 20th century is noticeably less than in the 16th century. Hambledon Hill, Dorset and Watlington Hill, Oxfordshire are also fine Yew forests. The latter is within an estate belonging to the National Trust.

A fine Yew in the Great Yew Forest – Earl of Radnor's Estate, Odstock, Nr Salisbury.

Great Yew Forest – Earl of Radnor's Estate, Odstock, Nr Salisbury.

Yew avenue – Close Walk Woods, Midhurst, West Sussex. Circa 1900.

Yew avenue – Close Walk Woods, Midhurst, West Sussex, 1988.

Yew Wood and the Longbow

The particular qualities of Yew wood have been recognised since pre-Christian times. Its specialist uses have varied from good to evil, from the stockade posts of the Druids, to spears and magic wands, from the pastoral crozier to the English Longbow. In addition, Yew has, since Elizabethan times, been noted for its value as a cabinet wood, especially for the supreme beauty of its curly tortuous grain. It is one of the finest woods available to the cabinet maker for veneer, and the special nature of Yew wood has also attracted the wood carver.

Yew wood is easily distinguished by the characteristic pink/brown colour of the heart wood, often highlighted by small areas of complex grain structure of a deeper hue. The cream coloured sapwood which may be from ¼ to 2½ inches in thickness presents a striking contrast.

Historically the Yew and the longbow are inseparable; so successful was the English archer in his use of the longbow that his fame spread across Europe. From the mid 12th century to the 15th century the longbow was the principle English weapon; both Edward I and Edward IV issued decrees requiring each Englishman to be in possession of a longbow of his own height and to be a trained bowman. In general, the European archers with their crossbows were no match for the English with their Yew longbows.

The superiority of the English archers lay primarily in their skill and astute technique which enable them to use the powerful Yew longbows with accuracy. No doubt this technique gave rise to the English phrase of 'bending a bow' and the French of 'drawing a bow'. The body weight was thrust behind the left arm in the centre of the bow, thus freeing the right hand for the accurate flight of the arrow.

Sir Arthur Conan Doyle paid tribute to the Yew tree in his *Song of the Bowmen*.

> What of the bow?
> The bow was made in England
> Of true wood of Yew wood
> The wood of English bows
> So men who are free

Love the old Yew tree
And the land where the Yew tree grows.

Before firearms came into general military use, the extensive use of Yew wood by the Bowyers resulted in a continuous decline in the number of Yew trees in our natural forests. This situation has never been retrieved, and the decline has continued; in consequence good quality Yew wood is now a scarce commodity. The exceptionally slow growth prevents planting as a commercial timber proposition, but its unique character always ensures it a place in parkland planting.

Because of the shortage of Yew wood, the latter part of this era saw Yew staves imported from Europe, particularly from Spain. An additional factor in favour of the continental Yew was its tendency to quicker growth, straight grain and freedom from knots.

Froissart's Chronicles graphically portray many of the battles in which the Yew longbow played a prominent part. In his report on the Battle of Blanchetagn, or passage of the Somme, which took place on the approach to Crecy, he reported:-

'The Frenchman defended so well the passage at the issuing out of the water, that the English had much to do. The Genoese did them great trouble with their crossbows. On the other side the archers of England shot so well together that the Frenchman were fain to give way to the Englishmen.'

In his chronicles on the Battle of Crecy which took place on the 26th August 1346, Froissart included in his narrative:

'There were of the Genoese crossbows about fifteen thousand, but they were so weary of going a-foot that day six leagues, armed with their crossbows, that they said to their constables, "We be not well ordered to fight this day, for we be not in this case to do any great deed of arms, we have more need of rest".'

When their plea was reported to the Count d'Alencon he charged them with being faint-hearted rascals. However, the count must have rallied his forces as the narrative continues:

'When the Genoese were assembled together and began their approach, they made a great leap and cry, to abash the English archers, but they stood still, and stirred not for all that. The Genoese again the second time made another leap and a full cry, and stepped forward a little but the Englishmen removed not one foot. Thirdly again they leaped and cried, and went forth till they came within shot. Then they shot fiercely with their crossbows. Then the English archers stepped forth and let fly their arrows so thick that it seemed snow. When the Genoese felt the arrows piercing their arms and breast armour, many of them cast down their crossbows and did cut their strings and retreat.'

Froissart also describes the prowess of Edward the Black Prince and his English archers at Poitiers in 1356 when they completely routed the steel-clad knights of France.

English bowmen also distinguished themselves at the Battle of Aljabrota in Portugal which was fought between the Kings of Portugal and Spain in the early part of the reign of Richard II. The King of Portugal was assisted by John of Gaunt, Duke of Lancaster with a force of English archers, each equipped with a Yew longbow. The King of Spain included in his force two thousand mounted knights from France with their crossbows. The chronicles in the language of the times describe how the English arrows pierced men and horses of the French and Spanish forces. So many lords and knights of France were taken they were unable to continue the battle.

Sir Thomas Brown must have had these battles in mind when he referred to the war-like Yew:

> The warlike Yew, by which more than the lance
> The strong-armed English spirits conquered France.

The rapid fire-power of approximately ten arrows per minute was also a substantial factor in the success of English archers in their battles with continental rivals. In 1346, the County of Kent included in their contribution to the war in France 100 longbows and 300 sheaves of arrows.

The 1982 raising of Henry VIII's famous ship *Mary Rose* – which sank in the Solent in 1545 with the loss of 700 men – was one of the most remarkable salvage operations of modern times. In addition to the main fire-power of 71 guns, the *Mary Rose* included in her armaments a number of smaller hand guns of different sizes. Of particular interest is the recovery, in good condition, of 168 Yew bows between 6 feet and 6 feet 9 inches in length, all carefully stored in purpose-made chests.

It is clear that the Yew bow continued to be a principle weapon of defence long after the introduction of firearms in the fourteenth century. Their recovery confirmed the selection process which must have been inherent in the widespread search for Yew bows to English longbow standard. Each bow was made from straight Yew staves preferably cut so that the bow consisted of both the pink heartwood and the white sapwood. The bow was then carefully fashioned to ensure the heartwood was on the inside, and the sapwood was on the outside, in order to make maximum use of the strength and elasticity of the Yew stave.

Yew forest on Hambledon Hill, Dorset – a view from across the Stour Valley.

THE COUNTRY

HOUSE YEW

Yew Avenue – Near Arklow, Ireland.

Chapter Five

The country house Yew, whilst not reaching the exalted significance of the churchyard Yew, does nevertheless figure prominently in a wide variety of situations ranging from the courtyard Yews of early manor houses to the Yew gardens of the great country houses of the 17th, 18th and 19th centuries. The Church and the Manor were two great influences on village lives. There existed between them a special relationship which continued through several centuries. Together with the Rectory and Rectory Farm, they were the main elements of the village coterie. In a similar way to its counterpart in the churchyard, one or more Yew trees were invariably found in a prominent place in the courtyard and gardens of the manor. Yew Tree Farm and Yew Tree House were common names for important village houses.

It became the custom for English farmers who provided food, accommodation and grazing for Welsh drovers on their way to the London market, to plant a group of Yew trees to signify their hospitality to the drovers. The trees also acted as way markers, and were used to mark resting places for travellers and pilgrims making their way to Canterbury.

The virtual immortality of the Yew and its association with the church gave the tree a special importance. It mirrored the desire for the continuity of a familiar scene and no doubt played a role in linking the past, not only with the present, but also with the future of the estate. They became a part of the established scene, to the extent that over the centuries some courtyard Yews acquired Biblical names such as Adam and Eve. The Emperor was another name occasionally given to ancient Yews of special significance.

Yew tree at Crom Estate, County Fermanagh – reputed to be the oldest in Europe.
© *(National Trust Photographic Library)*

One such tree prompted William Watson to write:-

> Old Emperor Yew fantastic sire
> Girt with thy guard of dotard kings,
> What ages hast thou seen retire
> Into the dusk of alien things?
> What mighty news hath stormed thy shade
> Of armies perished, realms unmade?

Prior to the middle of the sixteenth century, gardening activities were mainly limited to the orchard and to the kitchen garden, the latter providing an important source of herbs for medicinal purposes, salads and soups. The need to enclose and protect a large kitchen garden brought into use the Yew hedge; its screening qualities won praise from contemporary writers for the personal privacy it afforded to those able to wander away from the communal activities of the house. The herb garden was incidentally the original arbour, a name which continues to denote a secluded resting place in a large garden. These Yew hedges were described by Chaucer in the language of his time:-

> The hegge as thick as is a castle wall
> That who that list without to stand or go
> Though he would all day pryen to and fro
> He should not see if there was any within or no.

These herb garden hedges were the forerunners of the Great Yew hedges which were to follow in later years and reach the peak of their use in the eighteenth century.

A change of outlook destined to enhance the importance of the garden was materially helped by Italian craftsmen brought over by Henry VIII. Their advocation of larger gardens with a formal layout was initially only partly successful and in some instances seems incongruous alongside an English manor house. Support for the formal layout gained added impetus when the new era of country house building in the early Renaissance style began in the last quarter of the 16th century. This new building style ushered in the need for the allocation of land for a large garden to be developed and laid out in a manner to match the classical elegance of the great house. It became standard practice for the garden to be planned in great detail as an integral part of the Country House scene, and as a separate entity from the rolling parkland of the estate. This new approach to garden layout was also influenced by French and Dutch gardeners and further strengthened by a new generation of English gardeners.

Baddesley Clinton, Warwickshire, a National Trust, 14th century moated manor house with clipped Yews in the courtyard.

Avenues of trees, mainly lime, occasionally beech and Yew, were assimilated into the overall layout. Intricately designed beds of flowers, ornamental lakes, statues, pavilions, arbours, raised terraces with clipped Yews, Yew walks bounded by impenetrable Yew hedges, all found favour in many of the great gardens which complemented this new and fascinating age of Country House building. The total area of the house, garden and parkland was in many instances so large as to make the house remote from the village, but in practice estate maintenance ensured a strong link was maintained with the village and the church. The Dutch influence was primarily responsible for the great increase in topiary work. Clipped Yews were no longer limited to pyramids and columns; almost every type of conceivable shape from heraldic beasts to ships in sail was attempted and over the years accomplished. The novelty of these extremes of topiary work did not find universal acceptance. Some critics poured scorn on their work and referred to it as an absurd mutilation of the trees.

Little John — a quaintly clipped Yew.

Roadside topiary in the village of May Hill, Gloucestershire.

John Evelyn, who was the foremost writer of his time on trees, is generally credited as the first to bring the tall Yew hedge into fashion by making it a feature in his own garden at Sayes Court in 1617. Evelyn said he preferred them for their beauty, their perennial verdure and durability.

The gardens of the great country houses were a delightful visual experience; they encompassed every aspect of the gardeners art. The leading designers of this period were George London and Henry Wise. Their work included Hampton Court, Chatsworth, Blenheim, Melbourne Hall, and many of the large country house gardens. Yew gardens figure prominently in their work. Wise was later appointed superintendent of the Royal Gardens at Hampton Court and Kensington Palace.

During the first half of the eighteenth century there was a move away from the strictly formal garden, into a more open style with the grounds and the garden merging into parkland; fortunately the Yew walks and the clipped Yew hedges were retained. Yew avenues leading to the parkland were often included in this more open style.

Bridgeman made an important contribution to this trend by introducing the ha-ha, which permitted the garden to continue into the parkland without any apparent obstruction or break in the overall design.

The landscaped garden was further developed by William Kent (1685-1748) and his followers of that period. Later Lancelot Brown and his team completed the landscape style and in doing so altered or destroyed some of the fine formal gardens of London and Wise. Throughout these changes the Yew continued its distinctive role in both garden and parkland layout.

The judicious alignment of a magnificent Yew hedge with the house invariably enhanced its setting. It was nearly always the preferred choice to give shelter and privacy to the lawn in addition to providing a delightful dark green background. The Yew walk is another popular feature in castle and country house gardens. In its ideal form it will be around three hundred feet in length with each hedge consisting of two rows of Yews, staggered at three feet apart and trimmed to a height of between seven and ten feet.

Maintenance to keep the hedge free from holes and other blemishes is very skilled work; wiring, trimming, tying and occasional replanting are

A fine Yew at Dunkeld Cathedral lawns.

essential features of a maintenance programme. Yew hedges benefit greatly from an occasional dressing of a compound fertilizer; blood, fish and bone are eminently suitable as a Summer dressing. Nitrate of Soda given in late Autumn or early Spring is also helpful in maintaining the density of the Yew hedge. The vigour of the hedge can be noted by measuring the length of new shoots which in a healthy hedge will be ten to fifteen inches. Regular inspection should be made to check for the appearance of disease. As an aid to the avoidance of the spread of fungal attack such as Laetiporus Sulphureus, it is advantageous to dip cutting tools into a sterilant such as Ethyl alcohol.

Yew is ideal for the hedge maze, formal in appearance, dense, evergreen, easily trimmed and slow growing with a long life. The Yew maze at Hampton Court planted in 1690 is world famous. It survived the early 18th century alterations at Hampton Court at the special request of the King. It is the oldest maze in England and is still a major attraction to visitors.

In Jerome K. Jerome's well-known story *Three Men in a Boat*, he describes their desperate attempt to find a way out of the Hampton Court maze. Harris, one of the three, produced a map of the maze and soon had 20 people following him. Even with the map they remained lost and eventually shouted for the Keeper; he was having dinner, so sent the Assistant Keeper. He had great difficulty in finding them and was no better at finding the way out. Only the return of the Maze Keeper rescued the party.

Surprisingly, the glory of the Hampton Court garden is actually the magnificent avenue of clipped Yews; each is in the shape of a pyramid on a short clean trunk.

The World's largest maze is at Longleat House, the Seat of the Marquess of Bath. The design by Greg Bright is a magnificent achievement; it was opened to the public in 1978 and it consists of 16,000 Yews in 1¾ miles of hedge.

Blenheim Palace, the Seat of the Duke of Marlborough, possesses in its parkland a fascinating symbolic hedge maze portraying military features.

The Great Yew – Shugborough.

THE SHUGBOROUGH YEW TREE.

THIS is one of the most remarkable trees in England of its kind. It is noteworthy not only for its form and for the spread of its branches, but for the manner in which they have taken root and for the rapid growth of the young shoots after rooting. The dimensions are as follows: –

GIRTH AT GROUND	13*ft.*
HEIGHT	44*ft.*
CIRCUMFERANCE	300*ft.*
AGE	*about* 250 *to* 300 *years.*

Price 3d, including entrance to the tree.

Ticket for admission to Yew Tree – circa 1925.

The Great Yew at Shugborough

Shugborough Park is the magnificent 900 acre Seat of the Earls of Lichfield. It is now financed and administered by the Staffordshire County Council for The National Trust. The parkland contains many fine Yew trees in addition to clipped Yews which figure predominantly in the layout of the delightful garden.

One of the Yew trees is known as the Great Yew; John Lowe, writing in the *Garden Magazine* 1898, refers to this Yew as – *'One of the most remarkable Yew trees in England'*. He gives the tree dimensions: girth 10 feet 2 inches at 3 feet, the bole consisting of three trunks growing together up to 4 feet 9 inches, height 42 feet, diameter 87 feet and circumference 261 feet. At that time it was estimated at between 250 and 300 years old.

Clipped Yews at Shugborough.

Tall Yew in the gardens of Shugborough.

Adam & Eve – Speke Hall, Liverpool.

Its extraordinary growth has continued throughout this century. The current measurements are, girth 12 feet 3 inches, height 71 feet and the circumference is a remarkable 560 feet. The long horizontal low branches have taken root to form a dense circular hedge.

The copy of the ticket for admission to the Shugborough Yew Tree was purchased in 1925 by Mr Horace Roome, a footman at the Hall. A screen was erected around the tree, with a gate giving access to a passage reaching to the trunk.

Speke Hall, Liverpool, Merseyside

Speke Hall, 8 miles south east of Liverpool, is a remarkable Elizabethan Manor House, one of the most famous half-timbered houses in the country. The house is built around a central courtyard which contains two ancient Yews known locally as Adam and Eve. In terms of age they may pre-date the house. One entry in the records of the house states that in 1712 Ezekiel Mason was paid for making frames 'to set about Yew trees in the court'. They are probably between 450 and 600 years old. Although it is assumed they were planted at the same time, the girth of one of the trees is substantially less than the other. Speke Hall is administered and financed by The National Trust with the help of a grant from the National Museum and Galleries of Merseyside.

The Great Yew Hedge at Cirencester Park, Gloucestershire

The Bathurst Estate occupies 15,000 acres stretching westwards from Cirencester town centre through parklands to substantial woodlands and farms in the Cotswold Countryside. Under the guidance of Lord Apsley, the future 9th Earl Bathurst, it retains all the best characteristics of a traditional large country estate.

The magnificent Yew hedge is approximately 270 years old, and is in the shape of a huge semi-circle enclosing a grassy court. On its straight side this abuts the full length of the mansion, built around 1717 in the Queen Anne Style.

87

Hand clipping of the Great Yew Hedge at Cirencester Park.

(A daunting task before mechanisation)

The Great Yew Hedge at Cirencester Park.
(Clipping with the aid of mechanised equipment)

Because of its semi-circular shape, it is not possible from the outside to realise the magnitude of the hedge. The access to the courtyard through a small archway belies the striking impact of the full glory of a dark green 40 feet tall hedge which encompasses the courtyard like a protective deity. It is reputed to be the tallest Yew hedge in the world.

The width of the hedge at ground level varies from 20 feet to 23 feet. At the edge of the semi-circle, as is often repeated in other circumstances, the end Yew with no root competition on one side has a girth of 8 feet 10 inches. The average girth of the Yews in the hedge is approximately four feet. There are two rows of Yews with a minimum of five feet between trees.

In general they give the impression of a haphazard planting. Although in the early days sickly trees would probably have been replaced, in a maturing hedge this is impossible because of the bulk of the vigorous trees fills every available space.

The flat top is 15 feet wide, and the quality and closeness of the growth is such the foresters walk on the top with the aid of planks of wood.

Trimming carried out with the best modern equipment, takes two experienced men 10 working days. At the time of my visit, Jim Freeman was engaged on his 35th annual trim of the hedge, assisted by Tim Day who was jokingly referred to as an apprentice with eighteen years service. Pigeons are a problem – in gaining access they make holes which require branches to be tied and adjusted to fill the gap as part of the maintenance work.

Inside the hedge, which in part abuts a boundary wall, there is evidence that badgers and foxes have made use of it as a sanctuary in the past.

Mice, which shell the fallen Yew seed in Winter, have at times been a problem. Mice may have been responsible for an incident which nearly had disastrous consequences, when a cat working for the estate popped its head out of the hedge 20 feet from the ground immediately after the trimmer had passed by.

Packwood House, Lapworth, Warwickshire

Packwood House is a sixteenth century timber-framed house famous for its Yew garden. The house, gardens and estate of 113 acres belong to The National Trust.

Although parts of the garden date from the late seventeenth century it is likely that the bulk of the Yew garden was planted in the middle of the nineteenth century. It is not uncommon for Yews in country house gardens to acquire biblical names, and this practice was used at Packwood where the Yew garden is said to represent the Sermon on the Mount.

Twelve clipped Yews known as The Apostles in The Yew Garden at Packwood House, Warwickshire.

At the Northern end of the Yew garden is a flat-topped mound with a seat and viewing area around the master Yew tree. This area is reached by a spiral path from the Yew garden.

The walk towards the master Yew is flanked by twelve great Yews known as the Apostles, with four very large specimens in a central position. On each side of the Apostles is the multitude, these consist of varying sizes of clipped Yews, mainly shaped like tapering columns with

91

a flattish top. The grouping of such a large number of clipped Yews is very impressive; it is not a surprise that they acquired a biblical significance.

Blickling Hall, Aylsham, Nr Norwich

The garden at Blickling Hall, Norfolk is renowned for its great Yew hedges. An article in the *Journal of Horticulture and Cottage Gardener* in February 1873 refers to the front garden being bounded by a massive Yew hedge so common two centuries ago but now so rarely remaining. These Yew hedges measure 17 feet in height and 10 feet in breadth. They are known to be two hundred years old. It is interesting to note that one hundred and twenty years ago concern was being expressed about the loss of so many fine Yew hedges.

At that time the hall was The Seat of the Marquis of Lothian. It is now a National Trust property, and their desire to maintain and enhance the quality of the Yew hedges prompted the Trust to obtain a report in 1982 from John B.E. Simmons of The Royal Botanical Gardens, Kew.

One special feature of the Yew hedges at Blickling is the manner in which they align with the wings of the house to enhance the view of the southern façade of The Hall.

The hedge structure is impressive; each hedge consists of two lines of Yews, the older outer line hedge rising to 17 feet. The East hedge measures 290 feet x 15 feet and the West 301 feet x 16 feet. The report notes that fungal attack is responsible for the occasional loss of individual trees. Over the years approximately one-quarter of the original planting of 100 Yews at 3 ft intervals in each hedge has been lost. One large Yew at the South end of the hedge measured 6.5 feet in circumference, but in general the circumference of the Yews at 2 feet from the ground was less than 2 feet. The report outlined the need for regular maintenance including occasional dressings of a compound fertilizer (every three to five years) and the occasional application of an organic mulch along the outer faces of the hedges. If the mulch included manure then the fertilizer could be omitted.

Topiary doves at the entrance to the White Garden at Hidcote Manor,

Hidcote Manor Garden in Gloucestershire.

One of the features of Hidcote Manor is the Theatre lawn; after traversing the profusely planted gardens, there could not be a more restful scene. The long sweep of this close-cut lawn is bounded by a clipped Yew hedge, which provides a perfect dark-green boundary in contrast to the grass.

Clipped Yews are prominent in many garden areas; in particular high Yew hedges and topiary doves provide the setting for the entrance to one of the gardens known as the White garden. Hidcote is the "Mecca" for gardeners; it is owned and maintained by The National Trust.

Yew hedge providing the ideal background to the Theatre Lawn at Hidcote Manor.

Levens Hall, Near Kendal, Cumbria.

The gardens and park at Levens Hall remain as laid out in 1692. It is quite remarkable that the gardens, complete with their intricate clipped Yew topiary work, survived the 18th century desire for change to the landscaped garden.

Fortunately the present owners, Mr & Mrs Hal Bagot, and their gardeners have maintained the traditional appearance of the garden to the extent that it is often quoted as the finest example in Europe.

The panelled interior of the hall, the plasterwork and contents are quite exceptional.

Topiary garden – Levens Hall, Cumbria.

The Elephant Hedge – Rockingham Castle.

Rockingham Castle, Northamptonshire.

I visited Rockingham Castle following an exchange of letters with Commander Michael Saunders Watson D.L. As usual, the prime object of my visit was Yew lore, but this pursuit was overshadowed by the wonderful history of the Castle and the Watson family, whose association with the Castle dates back to 1540 when Edward Watson began the task of rescuing it from dereliction.

Yew trees are well represented within the castle garden. Clipped golden Yews figure prominently in a formal layout, and a high Yew hedge shelters the circular rose garden; in addition there are several individual Yew trees in the grounds. However, it is the massive Yew hedge known as the Elephant hedge and the Yew walk which are rather special.

So far as can be ascertained the Elephant hedge dates back to Tudor times – it consists of two lines of Yew trees cut to an unusual undulating profile, probably to accommodate the differing sizes of the trees making up the hedge. Charles Dickens was a frequent visitor to Rockingham, producing and acting in plays in the long gallery. He is said to have seen the ghost of Lady Dedlock pass between this old Yew hedge and disappear at the iron gates which lead to the wild garden.

Murthly Castle, Perthshire.

Whilst searching for information about the location of Yew trees of special significance, I noticed a very impressive photograph of a Yew Avenue, printed in a school-type Countryside book. The caption to the photograph referred to a fine Yew avenue in Perthshire, and it looked so attractive that I was determined to discover if it still existed, and if so, its location. This assignment did not prove to be a difficult one, as a very helpful director of the Tourist Office in Pitlochry advised me to inquire at Murthly Castle, as he felt sure that the photograph was taken within the castle grounds.

Following a letter and telephone enquiry, arrangements were made to visit, and it seemed prudent to link this journey with a visit to the Kirk at Fortingall, at the entrance to Glen Lyon – reputedly the longest, loneliest

The Yew avenue linking the Castle to the Church — Murthly Castle.

The author measuring the height of the Yews at Murthly Castle with a pocket surveyor.

and loveliest glen in Scotland. The Yew tree within the grounds of the Kirk is generally recognised to be the oldest living tree in Europe.

It is inevitable that when a long journey is made to record particular Yew scenes, the vagaries of our fickle weather are very much in mind. I recall anxiously looking out of the bedroom window of our hotel at first light near Dunkeld, only to witness a thunderstorm, and the rain beating on the panes with the ferocity of kettle-drums.

Fortunately this was short-lived, and the gloom soon hurried away, giving way to white fleecy clouds, fitful sunshine, and the unsullied clarity of air associated with this type of weather.

The two mile drive to the castle – which occupies an idyllic position high above the south bank of the River Tay – is through woodlands which immediately convey the impression of a well-cared-for estate.

On reaching the castle, we were greeted by Mr Stuart Fotheringham, the present Laird, who related to us the fascinating history of the Yew Avenue, and the legends associated with it. The courtyard and terraces which flank the castle are linked to the family kirk via an avenue, formed by seventy close-planted Yew trees around 60 feet in height with girths from four to eight feet, the whole setting is superb. Within the avenue, in the half-light of the dark green tunnel, a feeling of history and reverence is invoked that is quite different from any other type of tree-lined avenue. The presence of red squirrels also enhance the scene.

The Yew Avenue is also known as the 'Dead Walk', from a centuries-old custom that is still strictly adhered to – that the Laird shall only walk the avenue in the direction from church to castle, and the only journey made in reverse will be in his coffin!

Yew trees play a prominent role in the layout of the garden. In addition to magnificent specimens on the lawns, that are contiguous to the castle, there is a fine Yew Terrace, and also a well-kept Yew Hedge affording shelter to the herb garden.

Abbotsford, Nr. Melrose.

The parkland at Abbotsford, which includes trees planted by Sir Walter Scott, is in an attractive setting by the fast-running waters of the Tweed. The interior of the house itself is of exceptional interest in style and content. It is unchanged from the times when such distinguished contemporary writers as Thomas Moore and William Wordsworth visited Sir Walter.

Clipped Yews in the South Court Garden at Abbotsford.

In my search for information about the Yew hedges, Patricia Maxwell-Scott, a descendant of Sir Walter, and daughter of Major General Sir Maxwell-Scott of Abbotsford, was very helpful. She was able to outline the history of the Yews which were planted in 1860 by her great grandfather, James Robert Hope-Scott Q.C. The formal clipped individual Yew trees within the South Court garden provide an ideal period setting to the front of the house.

On the opposite side and parallel to the Tweed the Yew boundary hedge is several hundred yards in length – annual trimming by the gardeners must be a major task.

Buckland Abbey

Yew trees in the sunken Yew walk rising above the 60 feet high tithe barn.

Sir Walter Scott had apparently noted a 50 feet tall Yew tree on the farthest bank of the river and makes reference to its presence in *Rokeby*:

> To where the bank opposing showed
> Its huge square cliffs through shaggy wood,
> One prominent above the rest
> Reared to the sun its pale grey Breast,
> Around its broken summit grew
> The hazel rude and sable Yew.

Buckland Abbey, Yelverton, Devon.

Buckland Abbey was built by the monks of the Cistercian Order in 1278 and remained in their use until the Dissolution of the Monasteries in 1539.

The property was later bought from the Crown Agents by Sir Richard Grenville and subsequently converted into a Country Mansion by his grandson. However, its lasting fame is due to Sir Francis Drake, one of our greatest national heroes, who bought Buckland Abbey in 1581 and made his home there for the rest of his life.

All the main items of Drake personalia are carefully preserved including his famous drum.

The setting of Buckland Abbey in a sheltered Devon valley is superb. The mystical quality of the Abbey and its historical associations are enhanced by an avenue containing many fine Yew trees. They add a unique character to the Abbey and its adjacent magnificent tithe barn.

The Abbey and its estate are now in the ownership of the National Trust and maintained by Plymouth City Council.

There is a particularly fine Yew tree in the churchyard near to the entrance of the neighbouring church of Buckland Monachorum, which was closely linked to the Abbey. The rifle-straight growth style of this Yew with its attractive narrow fluted trunk must have received an approving glance from Sir Francis, who frequently worshipped there.

A fine Yew with a trunk free from low branches at Buckland Monochorum Churchyard.

Knockdrin Estates, Co. Westmeath, Ireland.

As in England, there has been a gradual reduction over many centuries of wild Yews in Ireland, although there still remain many fine specimens in Estate woods and parklands. The photographs include Yew trees at Knockdrin and Avondale.

The Yew and the Juniper are the only two conifers native to Ireland. They are dissimilar in many ways, Juniper being a small tree, rarely exceeding 20 feet in height. Several Irish and Scottish place names end in 'ure', a name derived from Gaelic and indicative of the presence of Yew trees, e.g. Glenure is the "Yew Glen".

In common with Oak, Yew is occasionally found in peat bogs, and in County Westmeath I was able to see bog Yew being recovered from peat excavations.

A fine Yew at Knockdrin Castle, Co. Westmeath, with a dense circle of branches down to ground level.

105

A tall Yew in the gardens of Avondale House, Wicklow, Ireland.

Sheldon Manor, Chippenham, Wiltshire.

Sheldon Manor is a medieval manor house which seems to have an atmosphere which brings history to life; it is fully lived in and has a warmth and friendliness which is enhanced by the owners Major Martin Gibbs and Mrs Elsie Gibbs.

Part of the house dates from 1282, including the great porch. Two fine ancient Yew trees are astride the path leading to the Porch; they admirably match the scene.

Yew trees at the approach to the entrance to Sheldon Manor.

THE CHURCHYARD

YEW

A fine Yew, one of several along the church walk at Kingham Church, Oxfordshire.

Chapter Six

There is a wealth of fascinating history enshrined in our village churches, and a look at a Church Visitors' Book with its liberal sprinkling of overseas visitors, will give an indication of the interest they excite.

Pagan sites of worship were, in general terms, circular in outline; it was a shape which continued in use throughout the Saxon period. One factor which helped the retention of the circular site was the mission of St Augustine in 597, who converted the pagan temples to the Christian religion.

Several circular churchyards are still in use; Deerhurst in Gloucestershire is a good example; part of the church dates from 804. Also in Gloucestershire, the Norman Church at Hewelsfield has retained its original shape.

Several exist in Wales, including a small churchyard at St Illtyd, Llanelltyd, near Dolgellau, where an interesting note about God's Acre and its sanctity is displayed in the church.

A church with a special historical significance may also have one or more ancient Yew trees, which add serenity to the church scene. In some instances the church will be in the centre of the village alternatively it may be outside the village and off the beaten track, a few may be isolated, the village having been abandoned in a Middle Ages plague epidemic and subsequently demolished. Usually the church tower acts as a guiding beacon; alternatively it is appropriate for the traveller in search of Yew lore to ask for directions to the church instead of the Yew tree. Otherwise there is a danger of directions being given for Yew Tree Farm, Yew Tree House or Yew Tree Inn.

THE CHURCHYARD

THIS is one of one of the very few churches in Britain with a circular graveyard. The church is built in the centre of this circle and any fugitive from justice securing a footing within the circle could claim sanctuary for seven years and seven days. The limits of the circle were settled in this way. A ploughman stood at the foot of the altar with his arm outstretched, and in his outstretched hand he held the yoke of his plough team. A plough team consisted of eight oxen, yoked two abreast, and the yoke extended from the front of the first couple to the end of the plough. Holding the yoke in his hand, the ploughman, no doubt with assistance, swept it round in a circle and all the land within that circle became holy ground. This is the origin of the phrase 'God's Acre.' It was the immediate circle of God's protection, not of the dead, but of the living, however ───── guilty ─────

Note framed and displayed in St Illtyd Church, Llanelltyd, Near Dolgellau.

A King Edward 1 Yew at Little Bedwyn, Wiltshire.

The esteem attached to the Churchyard Yew is quite impressive. Edward I and Richard III and Elizabeth I all issued decrees requiring Yew trees to be planted in Churchyards.

A notable Yew at St. Michaels, Little Bedwyn, Wiltshire has been continuously known through the centuries as the Edward I Yew and was presumably planted to comply with the King's decree, to help protect the Church from the elements. It stands near the Churchyard entrance, and South West from the Church porch.

Badger set under a Yew trunk with the added benefit of the sanctity of a Gloucestershire churchyard.

St. Nicholas, Oddington, Gloucestershire.

I particularly recall a request to survey a small parcel of woodland contiguous to the eleventh century church of St. Nicholas at Oddington, Gloucestershire. The churchyard is bounded by broad-leaved woodlands on two sides and they are linked together by a rather thin shelter belt which had the advantage of providing delightful views over Evenlode Vale to distant hills. A narrow lane of about a quarter of a quarter mile connects the church to the village. Originally the village was alongside the church, but it was moved in Medieval times to its present location, for no recorded reason. Perhaps it was due to the Black Death, or perhaps it was just enterprise, as the new village was sited astride the then developing turnpike road, to become an important staging post with six inns, stabling and horse changing facilities.

The nature of the siting of the church is not unique. Many Cotswold churches are set aside from the village and benefit from their limited isolation.

After completing the tree survey and making the required ground measurements, I made my way to the low stone boundary wall and climbed into the churchyard. The beautiful church of honey-coloured Cotswold stone, fortunately escaped the attention of the 19th Century church restorers; its medieval features are intact. The thirteenth century bell tower at the east end of the South Aisle should survive for another seven hundred years. Old memorial stones are hospitable to lichens which thrive in the pure air and provide a decorative pattern of muted gold and silver whirls. Uncommon wild flowers have been spared the vagaries of modern farming and have created a natural reserve.

It is easy to drift back in time; for many centuries the churchyard was a meeting place for secular activities, local and national news would be exchanged, information about the arrival of the stage coach would be announced at the church porch and quickly spread to workers in the fields. News of national activities and momentous occasions at home and overseas would be similarly dealt with.

During recent years an inborn desire to trace family roots often leads to people from the Commonwealth and America visiting country churchyards. I remember one occasion which achieved the desired result

Heythrop Old Church.

in quite a dramatic way. The lady came from Illinois; she had carried out protracted searches which had led her to believe that it would be advantageous to search the churchyard at Heythrop in Oxfordshire. She was staying with friends nearby and graciously accepted my offer to take her there. We found the church to be large in relation to the small village, with a green surround but no burial ground. There was nobody around to offer information about the church, so we began to assume it was Heyford churchyard we should be searching for, and not Heythrop. However, we were attracted to a bridle path which led away from the church towards one of the many spinneys which dot the countryside in this area. To our surprise, the spinney turned out to be Old Heythrop churchyard, with its church still intact but apparently abandoned as an active church. The churchyard was so overgrown that it was difficult to read the names on the memorial stones, especially those situated under a massive Yew which dominated the scene like a protective deity. Eventually, to our joy we were able to locate the memorial, and verify the family link with names and dates. I sketched the scene and later reminded her of the search in the following illustrated verse:

From Illinois to Heythrop

Tracing roots across the sea
Ancestral links are drawing me
Letters records, archives, the darkness is through
A century back in time, yet strangely new.

To old Heythrop Church by dry ditch and hedgerow mound
A bridle path to a lone burial ground
Velvet green moss, mole skin deep
Tombstones leaning, tombstones fallen,
The abandoned church asleep.

Ringed by departed souls
Just names on ancient parish rolls
An eerie secret scene
Silent and serene.

As inscriptions are scanned we are guided anew
To a rayless plot moist with dew

Hearts quicken as we look, it's there, it's true
The long search ends, in half light
'neath the Churchyard Yew.

St. Helen's Church, Darley Dale, Derbyshire.

The Yew tree at St. Helen's Church, Darley Dale, in Derbyshire, is a particularly well-known tree. It dominates the area between St. Helen's Church porch and the Churchyard entrance.

This ancient Yew is an integral part of Darley Dale history. Local belief is that its size indicates that the tree is over 2000 years old, which would make it an ancient Yew even in Saxon times.

An interesting plaque on the protective iron rail surrounding the trunk is a reminder of a few of the historical events likely to have taken place within its shade.

One of the incidents recorded in local history, and also related to me by a descendant of the same family, refers to a serious accident in 1711. A young man called John Gill fell off St Helen's Church roof after having gained easy access via the limbs of the massive Yew. In order to prevent similar accidents to local boys, some parishioners advocated the lopping of those branches over-reaching the church roof. Eventually their persistence, supported by later generations and no doubt other instances of church roof-climbing, was successful 95 years later, in 1806, the offending branches were severely lopped, resulting in a substantial loss of area covered by the branches, and also a change in the natural configuration of the tree.

The measurement of the girth of ancient Yews by different persons can produce conflicting figures. This is largely due to the irregularities in the shape of the trunk, with the result that a girth at 4'0" may be substantially more or less than a girth measurement at 3' 0" depending on the particular shape and height of the contortions and excrescences.

The Darley Dale Yew was measured by Dr. Burgh in 1782 for parish records. Additional girth measurements were taken by John E. Bowman, a botanical writer, in 1836 for the Magazine of Natural History. Mr Paget Bowman, a grandson of the above writer, also took measurements in 1888.

PROBABLE AGE ABOUT 2000 YEARS.

But whatever may be its precise age, there can be little doubt that this grand old tree has given shelter to the early Britons when planning the construction of the dwellings which they erected not many yards to the west of its trunk. To the Romans who built up the funeral pyres for their slain companions just clear of its branches. To the Saxons, converted, perchance to the true faith by the preaching of Bishop Diuma beneath its pleasant shade. To the Norman masons carving their quaint sculptures to form the first stone house of prayer, and to the host of christian worshippers, who from that day to this, have been borne under its hoary limbs, in women's arms to the baptismal font and then on men's shoulders to their last sleeping place in the soil that gave it birth.

The plaque detailing the main events which have taken place during the lifetime of the Darley Dale churchyard Yew.

119

Yew tree in St Helen's churchyard, Darley Dale.

More recently in 1983 a St Helen's Church committee, with Mr Ernest Paulson as secretary, made a report on the tree and obtained girth measurements for parish records. The details are:

Girth Measurements

Year	Base	2′ 4″	4′ 0″	6′ 0″
1782	–	–	33′ 0″	–
1836	27′ 0″	27′ 7″	31′ 8″	30′ 7″
1888	27′ 0″	30′ 9″	32′ 3″	31′ 2″
1983	27′ 3″	30′ 6″	33′ 2″	31′ 4″

It is noticeable that at a height of 4 feet the girth measurements at a 200 year interval are almost identical.

St Cuthbert's Church, Doveridge.

Lying close to the Derbyshire county boundary on the east bank of the River Dove and only two miles from the Staffordshire town of Uttoxeter, lies the village of Doveridge.

The village church of St Cuthbert contains within its churchyard a very special Yew tree with a fascinating local history. The age of this tree is locally estimated at 1400 years. The girth of the trunk is 22 feet. Although now partially hollow it carries a massive spread of branches covering an area of 400 square yards. Many of the branches would sweep down to ground level if it were not for the support given by a system of timber props and runners which enable the Yew to provide an impressive sheltered walk from the churchyard entrance gates.

The romantic link of this Yew tree with Robin Hood, the 12th century outlaw, is chronicled in the Roxburgh collection of manuscripts narrated in the 14th century and now housed in the British Museum in London. The story is told of the betrothal of Maid Marion to Robin Hood beneath this very tree by the Vicar of Doveridge, or Dubbidge as it was then called.

The Old Yew Tree, the subject of I.V. Orfords poem.

The church walk under the Old Yew Tree.

Said Robin Hood, lady fair whither away
Oh! whither fair lady away
She said him answer, to kill a fair buck
For tomorrow is Titbury day.

When dinner was ended
Sir Roger, the Parson of Dubbidge
Was sent for in haste
He brought his Mass Book, and
He bade them take hands,
And joined them in marriage full fast.

Titbury is the nearby village of Tutbury which in those days was an important place with a priory and castle.

Whilst on our Yew lore tour of Derbyshire we stayed at Matlock. I recall going back to Doveridge on a Saturday morning to retake a photograph in better light and immediately being enlisted to help in the preparatory work for a church fete.

The Doveridge Yew held a special interest for the poet I.V. Orford. His meditation under this ancient Yew reflects on life's changing scene:

So long and hot the way, the sun so bright,
I reach the church at last, to rest beneath
The branches of this Yew, and Lo! 'tis night.
No sun can pierce this comfortable shade
And these propped branches seem to bless the place,
Where tired bodies sleep in rest well earned
As babes they passed beneath its shade
For grace received at baptism, then as children
Laughing or grave, trip quietly on their way.

Then bridal pairs, shy and demure they pass
For the Church's blessing on their love to pray
Then later with slow steps they tread again
The way of life, so often trod, with mirth
At length the spirit fled far over the Yew
Their friends kind hands, have laid them earth to earth

So the old friendly Yew has seen them pass
A long procession's shadow on the grass
And I am dreaming in the gentle shade
Of giant branches swaying o'er the grass
Deep branches propped with timber so that we
Who walk in life may pace beneath their shade
And here a lantern hangs,
To light our way on darkening nights
As we go in to pray
That with God's truth our going we might stay

On hot days how grateful is the shade
These great dark branches give
Seeming to bless with shadows moving
As in soft caress, those who in earth's strong fold
Have gone to rest.

The Church Preen Yew, Shropshire.

It is perhaps understandable that before the time of travel by motor car, many villagers saw their ancient Churchyard Yew as so great a tree that they became convinced that it was probably the largest Yew tree in the Country. Church Preen and its Yew are an example of this.

Arthur Sparrow in *The History of Church Preen (1898)* referred to the tree's measurements – a girth of 24' 9" at 4' 0" from the ground and an umbrage of 230 feet, and added "it is indeed the glory of Preen".

It was from these details and up-to-date information on the tree from Mr A. Trevor-Jones of Preen Manor that I put the Church Preen Yew firmly on one of my Yew travels. I found it was not easy, as the adjacent area seemed to be a maze of minor roads of little more than single track width.

However, it was worth searching for. Its idyllic location matched the quality of this ancient Yew. The tree has been hollow since the earliest records were taken. One early report refers to the hollow portion being able to accommodate 21 men but adds they were standing upright.

Clearly in its life-span of over 1000 years it has sustained the loss of major branches, and as is common with many ancient Yews, the response from the vigorous root stock has been to produce new growth to make up for the losses.

Measurements at 4 feet from the base are:-

1780	19 feet
1833	22 feet
1889	22 feet
1897	24 feet 4 inches
1988	24 feet

In addition to the normal growth on the circumference of the trunk, there is evidence of new growth over the past century within the central hollow portion of the trunk. An iron band surrounds the trunk; it was probably placed there in the last century and is now restricting new growth on the periphery.

Trunk of the Church Preen Yew.

The young Yew at Ulcombe churchyard.

All Saints Parish Church, Ulcombe, Kent.

The Church at Ulcombe was established between 1213 and 1215 by the Archbishop of Canterbury as a collegiate church. The imposing tower was built in the 14th Century and alterations to the chancel are also of this period. The Church is larger than one might expect in a small village; no doubt this reflects its early days as a college. It is still a very special place. In addition, the churchyard has two magnificent Yew trees.

They are known as Old Yew and Young Yew. The Young one, 27 feet in girth is probably aged around 1000 years; it is safe to say the other one, 36 feet in girth, is much older. It has, during the last century, lost some of its main branches. This gives it a ragged appearance and adds to the contorted shape of the trunk where new growth has overtaken and fused with the damaged areas.

It must have been a magnificent tree in medieval times and no doubt the stonemasons would have used the tree for shelter and shade when building the Church. On my visit The Rev. Keith Chare was my helpful host; he noted that in the Churchwardens' accounts in 1722, Goody Rogers was paid 2d. for watering the Yew tree and a further 2d. for similar work in 1723.

Rugged splendour of the Old Yew, Ulcombe churchyard.

An exceptionally fine Yew, probably around 1000 years old, can be seen at St. Mary's churchyard, Selborne, Hampshire. This tree is delightfully situated on the North side of the church walk. Unlike many ancient Yew trees, its partially supported lower branches are of sufficient height to permit easy access and also adequate light to a circular seat which completely rings the 27' 0" girth.

I arrived at Selbourne on a hot July day when the cool shade of the Yew contrasted sharply with the heat of mid-day sun. There was a serene timelessness about the scene; in such a tranquil setting it seemed right to contemplate some of the unique fragments of local and national history which had been in one way or another linked to the life of this stately tree. It would have been a substantial tree in 1086 at the time of the survey for the Domesday book, which makes specific reference to Selbourne church and gives the name of the priest at that time at Radfred. The church on the site in 1086 was replaced by the present one around 1180.

In medieval times the churchyard was used for all manner of activities; it was in many respects the most important parcel of land in the village and often served as a meeting place. Important announcements would be made about a wide variety of events, from momentous occasions overseas to the date of the next Market day. In addition, activities ranging from archery practice to secular business deals would take place. Throughout all these events and affairs the Yew would be the focal point in the churchyard.

Gilbert White, 1720-1793, also put Selborne on the map; his book, *The Natural History of Selborne*, published in 1789, is universally considered to be an English classic. White makes particular reference to this Yew in the fifth letter of the *Antiquities of Selborne* where he says that in the churchyard of the village is a Yew tree whose aspect bespeaks it to be of great age. It seems to have seen several centuries old and is probably coeval with the church, and therefore may be deemed an antiquity. The body is short, squat and thick, and measures twenty-three feet in girth. White continues "This is a male tree which in the spring sheds clouds of dust and fills the atmosphere with farina."

The above paragraphs are my notes of a visit to the Church of St.

The Yew at St. Mary's, Selborne – before the storm.

The Yew at St. Mary's, Selborne – after the storm.

The stain glassed window which shows St. Francis preaching to the birds and includes the Yew tree.

Marys, Selborne following some interesting correspondence and helpful information from The Rev. John D. Curtis.

Alas, this fine tree was blown over and almost completely uprooted by the tremendous gale which swept this area on the 25th January 1990. Mr John Whitehead, a lecturer in Arboriculture, was instrumental in trying to save the life of the tree. The trunk has been winched back into position following the removal of the branches.

The easternmost window of the south wall is filled with a very fine three-light stained glass window representing St. Francis preaching to the birds. The birds can be identified as all of those mentioned in White's book; in the background can be seen the Church, the Churchyard Yew and the old vicarage where the naturalist was born. The window was paid for by public subscription in 1920 to mark the bicentenary of the birth of Gilbert White. It was the work of two Nottingham artists, Gascoyne and Hinks.

St. Peters, Hurstborne Tarrant, Hampshire.

Less than 25 miles from Selborne is the equally ancient Church of St. Peter's, Hurstborne Tarrant. Here the parish register has been kept with great care; one entry of particular importance, records on October 10th 1741 the planting of two Yew trees by the order and at the expense of James Wilkins MA, vicar of this parish. It is advantageous to have such clear documentary evidence of existing Yew trees. A visit on the 248th anniversary of their planting confirmed their excellent condition. Each with a girth of 9' 2", they are well-proportioned and situated in positions which enhance the setting of this beautiful church; its chequered history dates back to 1180 when the present church replaced an earlier one probably on the same site.

Jane Austen, William Cobbett and Ann Lee Merritt, the artist, all had strong ties with Hurstborne Tarrant and St. Peter's Church. William Cobbett wrote much of his reforming book *Rural Rides,* whilst the guest of Joseph Blount, a well known Hurstborne character. His massive flat tombstone lies between the two churchyard Yews; tradition has it that because of the lack of flat areas in Hurstborne Tarrant, he ordered his

The Parish Register records this Yew tree was planted October 10th 1741 in St. Peter's churchyard, Hurstborne Tarrant.

tombstone to be big and flat enough for the village children to play marbles upon it.

Hurstborne's steep hill presented difficulties to horse-drawn traffic, but not apparently to Joseph Blount's famous horse, Tinker, whose job it was to give the additional horsepower necessary to draw wagons up the steep hill.

Joseph and Tinker achieved local fame; one story recalls that at a parish meeting he was in a petulant mood and expressed his intention of being buried not in the churchyard, but under the local sheep-wash bridge "with old Tinker atop so the devil can't find me," which brought the reply, he was a fool if he thought the devil did not know the difference between a horse and an ass.

St. Gabriel, Stoke Gabriel, Devon.

One of the joys of searching out notable churchyard Yew trees is that invariably the church, the location or the village history offer the visitor an additional absorbing interest and pleasure. At Stoke Gabriel, the setting of the church of St Mary and St Gabriel high above a tidal stretch of the River Dart is superb with delightful views both upstream and downstream. The scene is further enhanced by a patchwork of woodlands and grasslands reaching down to the water's edge.

The churchyard Yew is a particularly fine specimen; the 17′ 9″ girth of its bole is sheltered by a huge umbrella of branches, and a low circular stone wall around the tree serves as a focal point and meeting place for several footpaths.

Close by the Church gates is the Church House Inn, a charming old village inn where the traveller immediately feels welcome. On a cold December day there is the additional warmth from a brisk burning log fire set in a huge stone fireplace. The Inn Keeper and two genial locals suggested it was the largest Yew in the country or perhaps the second largest; finally we all agreed it was the finest in the South-West.

Yew tree – St. Mary the Virgin churchyard, Stoke Gabriel, Devon.

St Mary The Virgin, Painswick, Gloucestershire.

The Churchyard of St. Mary the Virgin, Painswick, Gloucestershire is well known for its Yew trees but not in this instance for their age or size. Within the churchyard there are ninety-nine neatly clipped Yews; the majority are concentrated alongside two main paths leading to the church with the remainder dotted about the grassed area, between a unique collection of Renaissance and Baroque tombs of the 17th and 18th centuries.

Most of the trees are about 200 years old. Continuous clipping would seem to have reduced not only the natural growth, but also to have substantially inhibited the annual increase in girth. The result is that the bulk of them are under 3' 0" in girth, many of them being appreciably less than 2' 6", with a few of the larger specimens reaching over 5' 0" or thereabouts.

At Painswick, the Yew trees dominate the scene; this is particularly noticeable at dusk. In general, the history of Yew trees is often associated with a hint of mystery; it is perhaps inevitable that in the eighteenth century the figure of ninety-nine trees gave rise to the superstition that ill luck would be associated with the planting of one hundred trees.

The stout walls of the church tower, which was erected in 1480 still bear the marks of Royalist cannon shot fired during the Civil War in an attempt to drive out the Parliamentarians who had occupied the church. Although damaged, the church survived and continues to be very much in the forefront of life in Painswick.

In addition to the church, the other main legacy of the prosperity of the wool trade at Painswick is the delightful collection of large Cotswold stone town houses.

The Yews at Painswick are clipped around the third week in September in preparation for the church clipping ceremony on the following Sunday. It is a very old custom which has survived in Painswick. The local children encircle the church holding hands and swing into the church during the chorus of the ceremonial hymn:

O, that I had wings of Angels
Here to spread and heaven-ward fly;

Clipped Yew trees at Painswick churchyard, Gloucestershire.

I would seek the gates of Sion

Far beyond the starry sky

After the ceremony "clipping buns" are given to the children.

Hawling churchyard Yew around 65 feet in height, in an unusual situation on the boundary of the churchyard. It rises above the Sycamore in the Old Vicarage garden on the opposite side of a sunken lane.

139

A shady seat away from the mid-day sun at the Village Inn at May Hill near the Forest of Dean.

Some notable Churchyards in Kent.

Yew trees are particularly prolific throughout Kent. The majority of Churchyards possess at least one ancient Yew tree; many of these Yews are likely to be older than the church they shelter.

It is perhaps a little unfortunate that the presence of the Churchyard Yew is taken for granted. Churches are rebuilt, extended, altered and usually have a well documented record, but the Yew is rarely mentioned. This situation is at least partly the cause of the Yew trees mixed background of legend and history, stretching back to an era which revered it as part of a convocation of mystical rites and nature worship.

I made several visits to Kent and it was my good fortune that the Rector of Stowting, Monks Horton and Sellinge put me in contact with the local historian John Hammon of Stowting. In addition to proving an excellent guide, he was able to furnish me with details of local history and traditions. Our itinerary included Palm Tree Cottage, an old Tudor

140

Palm Tree Cottage, Stowting, Kent.

cottage in the village of Stowting. It is well known that in medieval Britain and some later periods, Yew branches were substituted for palm leaves in Palm Sunday processions. At Stowting, the information handed down through generations of villagers is that Yew branches were given out by the owner of a particular cottage, to be carried on the processional route to the church, with the result that the cottage became known as Palm Tree Cottage.

I have previously outlined in some detail the Yew trees unique capacity for new growth to achieve continuity of life. There are at least two examples in adjacent villages in South East Kent of a hollow Yew filling up with new growth. At Monks Horton the new trunk is growing vigorously within the hollow shell which still supports a substantial part of the umbrage. It is likely that within one or two centuries the new trunk will constitute the major part of the tree. New growth proceeds at a fast rate with the new trunk when compared with the branches from the outer shell; this is noticeable in so far as the shoots from major new growth areas will usually be about twice the length of the ordinary shoots e.g. 8 inches as against 4 inches.

The hollow portion of the Churchyard Yew at Stowting is also filling up with new growth. Richard Cobb, the Sexton during the first half of nineteenth century, records in his diary that the hollow Yew was used as a store for his tools. Since that time new growth has virtually eliminated this storage space.

It is now 20 feet in girth; increase in girth will continue to be limited but the filling of the hollow interior will continue and may eventually appear to coalesce with the older parts of the Yew on the periphery.

New growth inside a hollow Yew usually starts from the base of the tree, but instances do occur where the roots start from above the ground line.

Occasionally, when a multi-trunk Yew is cut down, it will be seen that the voids or cavities contain debris and roots. It would seem that the debris carried down from the crown of the tree by rain water stimulates root formation. In circumstances where there is a solid trunk below the voids, the roots will die. But when further decay extends the voids to ground level, the roots may continue to grow as normal roots and create a bizarre tree formation above the ground.

New trunk probably about 200 years old within the hollow trunk of an ancient Yew both growing in harmony.

A fine churchyard Yew at Brabourne, Kent.

The nearby Church at Brabourne possesses a particularly fine Yew with a very dense and wide spreading umbrage, and a trunk 15 feet 6 inches in girth.

Whilst in Kent I had the pleasure of meeting Rev. Donald Bish, the Rector of the Parishes of Wateringbury, West Farleigh and Teston, all within seven miles east of Maidstone.

The Yew at Wateringbury is one of very few trees with a recorded 16th century planting. Thomas Hood, a local man, planted this tree in 1597; it was also noted that it survived the great storm of August 19th, 1763, which caused tremendous damage to property and destroyed the bulk of the trees in the parish.

The 400 year old Yew at Wateringbury, Kent.

Old Yew and Young Yew at Stansted, Kent.

Unfortunately, its close proximity to the Church has resulted in the lopping of branches adjacent to the Porch. The trunk has a girth of 11 feet 4 inches.

My Kent journey included a visit to Stanstead Church. I recalled seeing its massive Churchyard Yew whilst training at the nearby Army Officer Unit at Wrotham. Although hollow, it is 30 feet in girth and supports an umbrage 60 feet in diameter. It was pleasing to see that a young Yew had recently been planted in a position between the Church and the entrance to the Churchyard. I noted the summer growth and the shoots of the young Yew were 15 inches long, and only 5 inches on the ancient Yew. With the Rector, Rev. David Clark, I discussed many aspects of the longevity of the Yew.

The traditional view at Stanstead is that their Churchyard Yew is 1,000 years old. The young Yew planted in 1982 should ensure that Stanstead has a Churchyard Yew for the next 1000 years.

Cudham Church near Sevenoaks has two fine Yew trees respectively 28' 0" and 27' 0" in girth. The Rev. Ian Leakey rightly considers them to be an important feature of the village. They are cared for by the Church Council through an expert tree surgeon.

St. John the Baptist Church, Tisbury, Wiltshire.

Tisbury is fortunate in being able to trace its history back to a henge monument or stone circle in what is now known as Cemetery Field. There is every indication that the pagan religion which included rituals associated with supernatural beliefs and tree worship gradually gave way to Christianity before the end of the Roman occupation. It is known that Constantine, the Roman Emperor in Britain in 306 AD, was a Christian; other early Christian activities are recorded on manuscripts in the British Museum, including details of a monastery at Tisbury in the year 672.

The church which in part dates from 1180 is within the scenically attractive area of the Vale of Wardour and close by the River Nadder.

There are a number of Yew trees in the Churchyard, including the well known ancient Yew which is situated near to the boundary wall on the North side of the church.

Concrete filling of the hollow Yew, Tisbury.

The hollow trunk has been filled with concrete, which also fills a gap in the 31 feet circumference of the tree. One inevitable result from the concrete filling, which may not have been appreciated when it was done, is that the area now available for new growth is reduced.

Where it is advisable to deal with problems arising from a hollow trunk, a programme of work which in general is worthy of consideration is:

(i)   Examine the tree for structural stability; then in the light of this examination give consideration to lopping, bracing and anchor props or any combination of these to improve stability. An additional factor to be considered is the need to have a balanced tree, not only to enhance its appearance but also to avoid unnecessary stress on the trunk.

(ii) Examine for fungal growth and if found take action to eliminate it with a suitable sterilant.

(iii) Consider improving the general health and vigour of the tree by adopting a feeding programme to encourage new growth, to consolidate and strengthen the trunk over a long term.

(iv) In some situations a ring of protective iron railings is desirable.

At Tisbury the present umbrage of the tree, whilst substantial, is less than the average churchyard Yew.

Whilst in the churchyard, I met an enthusiastic Campanologist and accepted his invitation to climb the tower to the bell frame, where he outlined the fascinating history of their peal of six bells. It includes a tenor bell of around one ton.

The Church of St. Mary & St. Peter, Wilmington, Sussex.

The ancient Yew in Wilmington Churchyard is a striking example of a twin trunk Yew; the low angle of its massive trunks gives the appearance of each having drifted away from the other to make room for their own massive array of branches.

In medieval times, the churchyard would often be a hive of secular activity; now, invariably, the churchyard is a quiet place, the tranquillity broken only by bird song, the drone of bees and an occasional grave tender at work with a trowel; usually, it is a lady working alone and happy to dispense some local historical information.

However, at Wilmington, the scene changed quite dramatically; just as I was making a close examination of the base of the trunk, a wedding party of around 100 left the church porch and made their way to the Yew tree. They took over the area around the Yew, whilst at least another dozen photographs were obtained. Here the Yew was in a different guise. Its presence added something special to the wedding ritual. It was a happy companion in much the same way as the Yew trees were regarded as happy companions in guiding the travellers on the Pilgrim way to Canterbury.

The Church is a mixture of architectural styles; several alterations and extensions have been made since its foundation in the 12th century. The Norman and Gothic styles blend well together in this small downland church.

A massive twin trunk Yew at St. Mary & St. Peter's churchyard, Wilmington, Sussex.

The well known Yew at Brockenhurst in the New Forest.

151

The Parish Church of St. Nicholas, Brockenhurst, Hampshire.

The church is delightfully situated on a mound which may be partially artificial. The Domesday book records the existence of a Saxon church; the outline of the circular churchyard can still be traced. The earliest part of the present church dates from around 1130. The great Yew tree on the South West side has long been an attraction to visitors to Brockenhurst. In 1793 its girth was 15 feet, in 1897 18 feet at 3 feet above ground level, and 18 feet in 1931 at a height of five feet from the ground; the current girth is around 20 feet. As regards growth and age estimation it is, for the reasons outlined in Chapter 2, unwise to read too much into the above figures.

In the print showing a view of the church in 1850, the Yew tree can be seen behind and above an oak tree which no longer exists. The shed on the left hand side is where the clergyman used to leave his horse.

The Brockenhurst Yew is likely to keep its age a secret but it is possible, bearing in mind that so many ancient churchyard Yews are broadly similar, that they it well have been planted in conjunction with the extensive church building which followed the Norman conquest.

The Great Yew Tree in 1850

152

A particularly impressive Yew at St Mary's Church, Overton, Clwyd, North Wales.

St Mary's Church, Overton, Clwyd.

Overton in the county of Clwyd lies close to the east bank of River Dee; it is within an area of the former County of Flintshire known as English Maelor. Overton is probably best known for the twenty-one ancient Yew trees which, in a dignified way, are dominant in the churchyard. These Yew trees are included in the seven wonders of Wales, apparently taking preference over the Gresford Yew only eight miles distant in a Northerly direction.

An old rhyme lists them all:

> Pistyll Rhaedr and Wrexham steeple
> Snowdon's mountains without its people
> Overton Yew trees, St. Winefrides wells
> Llangollen bridge and Gresford bells.

Part of the present church, including the tower, dates from the fourteenth century. An earlier stone church on this site was built towards the end of the 12th century. In all probability the Yew trees date from the time of the earlier church. The largest is a female tree with a girth of 17' 8".

All Saints Church, Gresford, North Wales.

The ancient Yew at Gresford is one of the best known trees in Britain. It has, over the past 180 years, been the subject of much speculation about its age. Estimates in the past have varied from 850 years to 1,734 years; they have been based on girth measurements, ring counts from bore holes, ring counts on decayed wood samples and, perhaps, imaginative perception.

It was noted that over a 41 year period of observation, the girth measurements were approximately three times greater than would be expected, considering the bore hole ring counts. During this period, the increase in diameter at ground level was 1.25 inches, at 2 feet above ground level 7 inches, and at 4 feet 6.15 inches. These and other results show the difficulty in estimating the age of an ancient Yew by this method.

The ancient Yew at All Saints church, Gresford.

I was surprised to read an account by a well respected historian referring to the Gresford Yew as solid to the core. In general, the ancient churchyard Yews are the product of a multi-trunk growth pattern, which is the precursor of the hollow trunk.

Tom Evans, a very knowledgeable local historian and former Verger and Sexton, put to me his view of the age of the Gresford Yew, based on his research and hypothesis relative to events in the Gresford area. He is strongly of the opinion that it was planted about the year 350 AD alongside the grave of a Roman Officer, by his widow. It is known that the Roman XX legion was stationed at Chester, seven miles to the North, and that an outpost of the legion existed close to Gresford. The Roman Officer connection is supported by an ancient carved stone found during the boiler house excavation work in 1902 and now preserved in the Church.

The carving depicts a female figure holding a pair of scissors; at this point in the story I had an uneasy feeling of danger, but Mr Evans explained the link between the carved figure and Greek mythology which exerted a religious influence at that time. Apparently, the three Atrophus sisters controlled the lives of all men who had reasonably pleasant occupations; one spun the thread of life; the second provided, from this thread, the tapestry of life for her husband and the third had the unfortunate task of cutting the thread at the appropriate time to end his life.

There is no reason to doubt that a Roman Officer's wife, at that period of time, would be familiar with mythology, which played a part in other aspects of the life of Roman soldiers.

The story continues with the carved stone being placed on the grave and a Yew tree planted nearby to ensure his immortality. Mr Evans believes that in the Reformation period, the stone was regarded as idolatrous and was discarded around 1536.

Fortunately, some of these events cannot be proved as right or wrong and the Gresford Yew is likely to keep its age a secret.

It is not unusual for ancient grave-covers and marker stones to be found during excavations on religious sites. In some instances, carved representations of foliage have been noted, signifying the importance of trees in earlier times. A good example of an early 10th century grave-cover of this type was found during recent excavations at St Oswalds, Gloucester and is now on display in the city museum.

The Church of St. Peter, Peterchurch, Hereford.

Peterchurch, twelve miles west of Hereford, is known locally as the capitol of the Golden Valley. The church of St. Peter on this site dates from 786 AD. About 1130 AD, the Saxon building was replaced by the present Norman church; fortunately, the original Saxon stone altar has survived.

According to church records, the churchyard Yew dates from the late thirteenth century. In medieval times, it was occasionally coppiced by the local bowyer.

Three Irish Yews at St. Peters, Peterchurch, Hereford.

Ancient Yew at St Peters Church, Peterchurch, Hereford.

Planted late 13th century.

The Rev. John Davies, the Rector, in making reference to the hollow trunk, mentioned that an army deserter in the First World War had used the trunk as a hiding place.

On a summer morning about 15 years ago, it was noticed that a fire was burning inside the tree; only a concerted effort with a bucket chain saved the tree.

It is pleasing to note that on St. Peter's day 1986, as part of the celebrations of the 1200th anniversary of the founding of the church, Bishop Cannon planted a little Yew near to the ancient Yew, ready to take over, if necessary, in future centuries.

Abbey Dore Church, Hereford.

The church of Abbey Dore lies in the golden valley of the River Dore seven miles downstream from St. Peter's Peterchurch. The church is immediately noticeable as a building vastly different from any other church. The history of the church is both remarkable and fascinating. Dore Abbey was built in this remote valley by Cistercian monks in the 12th century. Only fragments of the Abbey survived the Dissolution; it was in a ruinous condition when the remains of the abbey were granted to Lord Scudamore by Henry VIII early in the 17th century. He sought the assistance of the King's carpenter John Abell; together they carried out restoration work on the remaining parts of the abbey, rebuilt the tower and skilfully made Dore Abbey church with due regard to its Gothic past.

The new church was consecrated on Palm Sunday 1635; a lasting tribute to their work.

The churchyard Yew is in a prominent position alongside the path leading to the church porch. It is in good heart, somewhat younger than the Yew trees in many of our Norman churchyards. Its appearance strongly indicates that it was planted about the time of the dedication of the church.

Ancient Yew in Abbey Dore churchyard.

The Fortinghall Yew, Perthshire.

This famous Yew tree is in the grounds of the Kirk at Fortinghall, a village at the entrance to the romantic Glen Lyon, and is generally accepted to be the oldest living tree in Europe.

In size, it is less in height and umbrage than the average Churchyard Yew, but it does have the advantage of being in an area of exceptional natural beauty. Estimates of its age vary between 1500 and 3000 years; they are based on a girth of between 52 and 56 feet, but unfortunately, only fragments of the girth have survived. The living portions are healthy but a detailed inspection was difficult due to the substantial protective wall and railings, which have now been in place approximately 150 years.

The Fortinghall Yew, the oldest tree in Europe.

The age estimates can only be speculative; like all other ancient Yews, its trunk has followed the general pattern of evolution, production of sapwood, change of heartwood, followed by the decay of the heartwood until it ceases to exist. How soon the decay stage arrives depends on a number of factors; it is likely to be between 400 and 800 years of age but can

161

be much sooner. The Fortinghall Yew is an example of continuous new growth on the periphery of parts of the trunk, giving the tree an indefinite life span.

The Great Yew at Fortinghall

An 18th century print showing a funeral party passing through the centre of the Yew.

Although Fortinghall is only a small village, it has the right components; a kirk, a friendly hotel and a delightful setting amidst an area of mountains, locks and riverside walks. It was an important Roman Camp, reputed to be the birthplace of Pontious Pilate. It is an area which merits a descriptive note:

> This is the Scotland to cherish and know
> The country hotel with its evening glow
> Romantic Glen Lyon with the sound of its river
> Like the Fortinghall Yew may they live forever.

Harlington Church, Hayes, Middlesex.

There cannot be another churchyard Yew to match the chequered history of the Harlington Churchyard Yew. I am grateful to the Rector Rev. D. Jenkins and to Mr Philip T. Sherwood for the historical information associated with this tree.

The extraordinary topiary work practised on this Yew in the eighteenth century is graphically recorded in an engraving published in 1770 by the parish clerk. His publication also records the doggerel rhyme written by John Saxy in 1729 when he was responsible for the clipping and maintenance of the tree. The clipping was an annual task done prior to the Whitsun fair.

Towards the end of the eighteenth century, the shape seems to have been gradually modified; a print of 1803 shows the loss of some prominent features of the earlier topiary work and by 1840 it had been allowed to return to a normal growth pattern.

Small clipped Yews in cylindrical shapes are common in churchyards, but mature Yews have never been regarded as suitable subjects for topiary work. Although this fanciful style of decoration had its critics, there is little doubt that towards the end of the seventeenth century, topiary work in one form or another became an essential part of the gardener's work. This was partially due to the accession to the throne in 1688 of William of Orange, who gave prominence to gardeners who included in their schemes clipped Yews of ingenious shapes.

163

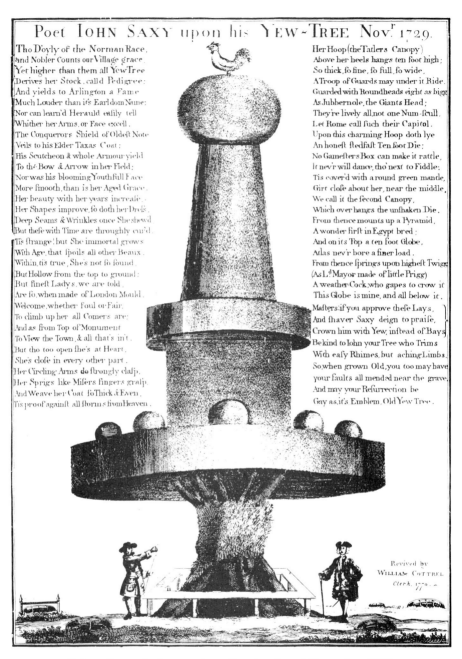

Extraordinary topiary work on the churchyard Yew, circa 1729

The Harlington Yew tree mid 19th century.
Has been allowed to return to a normal growth pattern.

There has been the inevitable speculation about the age of the Harlington Yew. The 1729 print and John Saxy's description points to a fine tree 60 feet in height with a girth of over 20 feet. When compared with Yew trees planted as a result of decrees by Edward Ist and also those planted in association with the extensive programme of church building in Norman times, the Harlington Yew is likely to be contemporary with the Norman period.

The Harlington churchyard Yew, October 1991 now recovering from severe storm damage.

The greatest tragedy in the life of this Yew tree occurred in 1959 when the effects of a severe gale reduced the tree to a mere stump of 12 feet. However, in true eternal Yew fashion it is recovering and producing a substantial amount of new growth each year.

The Yew at Wooland viewed from the church porch.

The Parish Church of Wooland, Dorset.

The old Yew tree which dominates the small churchyard at Wooland is probably the only Yew to have given shelter to three or possibly four churches. The present church was built in 1856, partially with the materials from the church it replaced, which was built in 1743 to replace an earlier church dating back to 1547. There may have been a Saxon church on this site or some place of worship, as it is recorded that Wooland was an outpost of Middleton Abbey in the tenth century. The Yew has a twin trunk; it is sometimes referred to as a split trunk, but this is a natural type of growth. In 1871, its girth was 23 feet; it is now almost 32 feet. With a height of 60 feet and an umbrage 58 feet in diameter, the Wooland Yew overshadows one half of the churchyard.

The Parish Church of St. Mary, Eastham, Cheshire.

The Church is pleasantly situated in the old village of Eastham. The church dates back to the 13th century.

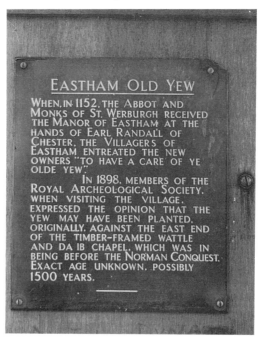

Notice outlining important events within the life of the Eastham Yew.

Churchyard Yew in the parish church of St Marys, Eastham, Cheshire.

The two aisles are divided from the nave by early 14th century arcades of four bays with octagonal pillars. The main feature of the church is 116 feet broach spine, which is a notable landmark.

Equally famous is their Churchyard Yew, which is often claimed to be the oldest Yew in Britain. It is a particularly fine specimen. In 1152, the villagers specially requested the owners "to have a care for ye olde Yew". It would seem to have been well cared for during the past 940 years. The girth at 4 feet 6 inches is 21 feet.

All Saints Church, Didcot, Oxfordshire.

All Saints Church dates from the 12th century, when the area was described as a well watered woodland. There is ample evidence of the Roman occupation, followed by a Saxon settlement. It is likely that a wooden church existed on the site of the present church.

The churchyard Yew is a rugged tree which may well pre-date the church. The girth is 23 feet 6 inches; it gives the impression of being a survivor whatever the circumstances – a typical eternal Yew.

Coln Valley, Gloucestershire.

The enchanting stretch of the Coln Valley from Fosse Bridge, four miles south of Northleach to Bibury is traversed by a winding country lane which passes through the hamlets of Coln St Dennis, Coln Rogers and Winson.

Each hamlet has a church of Norman origin and an imposing churchyard Yew.

At Bibury, where there is a delightful country hotel, the river has a stony bed which provides clear water in addition to rapid shallows and languid pools on its way to Coln St Aldwyns.

The village names emphasise the importance of the Church and the river in a past era.

Ancient churchyard Yew trees of special interest can also be seen at St

Ancient Yew at Didcot.

Mary and St Peter, Hayling Island; Long Sutton, Warblington; Corhampton, Hampshire; Crowhurst and Tandridge, Surrey; Crowhurst, Sussex; Great Berkhamstead, Hertfordshire; Totteridge village, London; Mamhilad, South Wales.

The churchyard Yew at Winson, Gloucestershire, sheltering the Norman church of St. Michael.

Also of historic interest is the Ankerwyke Yew, near Staines. Nineteenth century reports on this tree have referred to it as being hollow; it is interesting to note that during the past century there has been a substantial amount of new growth within the hollow centre.

Ankerwyke, which is in private ownership, was originally part of the former Priory of Ankerwyke.

Alan Merideth, who is closely involved in Yew lore, has carried out detailed research both on this Yew and the adjacent land areas which include Runnymede. He is of the opinion that this Yew may be a living link with King John and the Magna Carta.

The ancient Yew at Coln Rogers, Gloucestershire.

Yew trees giving shelter to the North Porch of St. Edwards Church at Stow-on-the-Wold, Gloucestershire.

A dense bushy Yew reputed to be around 1,000 years old in the churchyard at Allestree, Derby.

ADAM and EVE
or
THE EXPULSION GROUP
Carved by E.J. Clack, F.R.B.S.

The Yew tree grew in St. Paul's Churchyard, Tiverton and was felled in 1946 and work was then started on it.

The natural trunk suggested the subject and the carving was direct, i.e. no models were made. It was first exhibited at the Royal Academy in 1948 and was then exhibited in northern galleries in 1949

It was presented to the Bishop of Bath and Wells in 1963.

POSTSCRIPT

&

LIST OF YEW TREES
OF SPECIAL SIGNIFICANCE
EXTRACTED FROM THE TREE
REGISTER OF THE BRITISH ISLES

POSTSCRIPT

I recall the late Richard St. Barbe Baker saying what a delightful pleasure it is to visit famous trees and record their history. At that particular time, my travels had been of a modest nature, but this endorsement from a world-famous forester gave me encouragement to widen the scope of my journeys.

One delightful side effect of my Yew lore travels has been the pleasure of being able to meet and converse with persons in such a wide variety of situations; country churchyards, castles, mansions, parklands, gardens, Yew forests and wayside Inns. Many villages show a considerable interest in their churchyard Yew; in at least six villages, the message was that their churchyard Yew was the oldest in the country; an almost equal number thought their Yew might be the second oldest Yew.

I have not at this stage been able to visit all the places which have been the subject of invitations. This leaves the reader and myself in a happy situation of still being able to discover some equally fascinating Yew trees; invariably, they will be found in a place of beauty or of historical interest or perhaps both. They are an important part of our natural heritage, worthy of special care and maintenance in order to ensure that for many centuries, perhaps another millenium, they will continue to fascinate every person with a real interest in trees and the countryside.

As a further guide to the location of additional Yew trees of special significance, Alan Mitchell, a leading consultant on trees and related environmental matters, has kindly provided the following list taken from The Tree Register of the British Isles. This is a computerised revolution in tree recording in which he is closely involved.

Location	Height		Girth	
	ft		ft	ins
Bedhampton, Hants	52	x	21	6
Bedhampton, Hants	52	x	20	2
Steep, Hants	48	x	22	3
Breamore, Hants	25	x	35	0
Lockersley, Hants	46	x	26	6
Dursley, Hants	56	x	23	8
Boarhunt, Hants	33	x	26	6
Farringdon, Hants	36	x	30	4
Itchen Abbas, Hants	36	x	24	3
Hawkley, Hants	50	x	23	4
Prior's Dean, Hants	60	x	25	2
Buxted, Suusex	50	x	32	0
Crowhurst, Sussex	50	x	29	5
Etchingham, Sussex	52	x	21	3
Herstmonceux, Sussex	44	x	21	3
Cold Waltham, Sussex	40	x	31	0
Stedham, Sussex	30	x	30	7
Funtington, Sussex	33	x	21	8
Lavant, Sussex	36	x	22	3
Sullington, Sussex	40	x	21	1
East Chiltington, Sussex	50	x	22	1
Slaugham, Sussex	50	x	23	3
Warlingham, Surrey	40	x	22	3
Druid's Gr. Norbury	65	x	20	7
Hambledon, Surrey	60	x	32	6
Dunsfold, Surrey	42	x	25	1
Alford, Surrey	33	x	24	8
Cobham, Surrey	44	x	21	7
Keffolds, Haslemere, Surrey	48	x	29	0

Leeds, Kent			30	0
Loose, Kent	46	x	32	0
Elmstead, Kent	56	x	20	8
Elmstead, Kent	52	x	20	5
Godmersham, Kent	40	x	21	4
Hastingleigh, Kent	50	x	25	0
Dinder, Somerset	52	x	30	11
Broomfield, Somerset	50	x	21	2
Dinton, Somerset	56	x	22	5
Mamhead, Devon	23	x	33	0
Dartington Ch., Devon	46	x	25	0
Kenn and Kentford Ch.	60	x	37	0
Iffley, Oxon	25	x	23	1
Rycote, Oxon	46	x	24	5
Steventon, Berks	33	x	21	0
Churcham Pinetum, Glos	52	x	20	3
Bockleton, Worcs		x	23	7
Staunton, Worcs		x	32	0
Cusop, Herefords	40	x	23	3
Stanford Bishop, Hereford	42	x	23	1
Linton, Herefords		x	33	7
Norbury, Salop		x	34	0
Bucknell Ch. Salop	73	x	19	0
West Tisted, Hants	62	x	20	8
Caerhun, Gwynedd	42	x	23	8
Llanellyd, Gwynedd	50	x	24	1
Defynnoc, Powis	30	x	35	3
Defynnoc, Powis	40	x	24	0
Kelburn Castle, Ayrs.	56	x	17	3
Whittingehame, E. Lothian	50	x	11	9
Ormiston, E. Lothian		x	17	9

Ellon, Aberdeen	33	x	15	6
Lawers, Perths	50	x	17	3
Dundonnell, W. Ross	50	x	23	0
Tarbet House, E. Ross	40	x	15	3
Rossdhu, Dunbartons.	33	x	17	0
Glencormac, Co. Wicklow	56	x	21	0
Rosanna House, Co. Wicklow	30	x	16	0
Shelton Abbey, Co. Wicklow		x	18	0
Powerscourt, Co. Wicklow	46	x	12	9
Woodstock, Co. Kilkenny	70	x	12	9

The girth measurements have been taken at different heights, To take account of the nature of the individual tree. Where a tree has forked or changed to a multi-trunk growth pattern, the girth measurement has been taken below the visible change in growth style.

Trunk of an ancient Yew at Dryburgh Abbey, reputed to have been planted 1136 but almost certain to have been planted at a later date.

INDEX

A

Abbey Dore Church, 159

Abbotsford, 101

Age Estimation, 25-6, 28, 39, 152, 154, 161

All Saints Church, Didcot, 170

All Saints Church, Gresford, 154, 155

All Saints Church, Ulcombe, 128

Ankerwyke Yew, 172

Annual Rings, 25-6, 28, 30, 32-3, 154

B

Baxter Trevor, 20, 22

Bird Sown Yews, 47

Bish, Rev. Donald, 145

Blair, 18

Blickling Hall, 39, 92

Botanical Features, 41

Brand, Gordon, 11, 52

Bridgeman, 79

Bright, Greg, 81

Brockenhurst, 16, 151-2

Brown, Sir Thomas, 68

Brown, Lancelot, 79

Buckland Abbey, 102-3

Buckland Monachorum, 29, 103-4

C

Cabinet Wood, 66

Carbon Dating, 26

F

Fortinghall Yew, Perthshire, 161-3

Fotheringham, Stuart, 100

Freeman, Jim, 11, 90

Froissarts Chronicles, 67-8

Funeral Rites, 17, 19

G

Gibbs, Elsie, 107

Gibbs, Major Martin, 107

Girth Measurements, 26, 28, 118, 121, 154, 182

Glen Lyon, 97, 161, 163

Golden Yew, 50, 54, 97

Grave Covers, 156

Gray, Thomas, 19

Great Yew Woods,

H

Hammon, John, 140

Hampton Court, 79, 81

Harlington Church, 163

Herrick, Robert, 19

Heythrop Churchyard, 116-7

Hidcote Manor, 93-4

Hollow Trunk, 33, 148, 156, 159

I

Irish Yew, 50-1, 53-4

J

K

L

M

N

National Trust, 52, 61, 76, 83, 87, 91-3, 103

Native Evergreen Trees, 15-6, 26, 43

O

Orford, I.V, 124

P

Packwood House, 91

Painswick Church, 137

Palm Tree Cottage, 140, 142

Palm Sunday, 17, 142, 159

Paulson, Ernest, 121

Pilgrims Way, 73, 149

Plymouth City Council, 103

Poisonous Nature of Yew Leaves, 45, 46

Poitiers, Battle of, 68

Pontious Pilate, 163

R

Rockingham Castle, 97

Roxburgh Collection per Mr. F. Cope, 121

S

St Augustine, 111

St Barbe Baker, Richard, 179

St Cuthberts, Doveridge, 121

St Edwards, Stow-on-the-Wold, 174

St Elli, Llanelly, 16

St Erfyl, Llanerfyl, 38

T

Taxus Baccatta, 43, 50

Taxus Baccatta Dovostoniana, 50

Taxus Baccatta Elegantissima, 54

Taxus Baccatta Fastigiata, 50

Taxus Baccatta Lutea, 54

Tennyson, Lord, 18, 43

Todenham, Gloucestershire, 40, 46-7

Topiary Work, 76-8, 93-4, 163-4

Tree Register, 179

U

Unique Growth Style, 23

W

Walley, Mr. 11, 61

Wateringbury Parish Church, 145

Watlington Hill, 61

Watson, Michael, Saunders, 97

Watson, William, 75

Wheeler, Reg, 38

White, Gilbert, 129, 133

Williams, Conrad T., 16

Wise, Henry, 79

Wooland Parish Church, 168

Y

Yew – Clipped, 76-7, 79, 81, 83, 91-4, 97, 101, 137, 163

Yew – Cultivars, 50

Yew – Hedges, 75,79, 81, 88-90, 92-4, 97, 100-1